Michael Pollak, PhD

The Second Plague of Europe: AIDS Prevention and Sexual Transmission Among Men in Western Europe

*Pre-publication
REVIEWS,
COMMENTARIES,
EVALUATIONS . . .*

The comparative European perspective that has become possible thanks to Michael Pollak himself brings an essential addition to the AIDS literature."

Gert Hekma
Gay Studies,
University of Amsterdam

Pollak's posthumous book is a solid sociological analysis and also a personal example of both social and individual mobilization for fighting against a deadly disease."

Rommel Mendès-Leite, PhD
Sociologist and President,
Research and Study Group
on Homosociality and Sexualities
(GREH),
Paris, France

"*T*he Second Plague of Europe discusses the context of AIDS prevention and its instruments, analyzes methodologies of assessment research undertaken in Western Europe and their result in terms of behavior change, and discusses the successes and failures of prevention in regard to the epidemiological data.

Pollak gives us an overview of the AIDS epidemic. . . . On the basis of quantitative sociological and epidemiological data, he analyzes the differences and similarities between each European country considering either the socio-cultural perception of homosexuality, its legal status and the development of the gay movements, then the collective effort of the gay community to assess AIDS prevention.

"*T*he Second Plague of Europe convincingly documents that safer sex is a culturally differentiated process. The European countries differed in their approaches taken in the fight against AIDS. These differences are shown to relate to a variety of factors: national traditions, the presence and strength of an organized gay community, the level of coordination between formal and informal groups involved, the status of the medical establishment, the time at which preventive action began, and the stage of the epidemic.

The Haworth Press, Inc.

The Second Plague of Europe

*AIDS Prevention
and Sexual Transmission
Among Men in Western Europe*

HAWORTH Gay and Lesbian Studies
John P. De Cecco, PhD
Editor in Chief

New, Recent, and Forthcoming Titles:

Gay Relationships edited by John De Cecco

Perverts by Official Order: The Campaign Against Homosexuals by the United States Navy by Lawrence R. Murphy

Bad Boys and Tough Tattoos: A Social History of the Tattoo with Gangs, Sailors, and Street-Corner Punks by Samuel M. Steward

Growing Up Gay in the South: Race, Gender, and Journeys of the Spirit by James T. Sears

Homosexuality and Sexuality: Dialogues of the Sexual Revolution, Volume I by Lawrence D. Mass

Homosexuality as Behavior and Identity: Dialogues of the Sexual Revolution, Volume II by Lawrence D. Mass

Sexuality and Eroticism Among Males in Moslem Societies edited by Arno Schmitt and Jehoeda Sofer

Understanding the Male Hustler by Samuel M. Steward

Men Who Beat the Men Who Love Them: Battered Gay Men and Domestic Violence by David Island and Patrick Letellier

The Golden Boy by James Melson

The Second Plague of Europe: AIDS Prevention and Sexual Transmission Among Men in Western Europe by Michael Pollak

Barrack Buddies and Soldier Lovers: Dialogues with Gay Young Men in the U.S. Military by Steven Zeeland

The Second Plague of Europe

AIDS Prevention and Sexual Transmission Among Men in Western Europe

Michael Pollak, PhD

The Haworth Press
New York • London • Norwood (Australia)

The Haworth Press, Inc., 10 Alice Street, Binghamton, NY 13904-1580

Library of Congress Cataloging-in-Publication Data

Pollak, Michael.
    The second plague of Europe : AIDS prevention and sexual transmission among men in Western Europe / Michael Pollak.
       p. cm.
    Includes bibliographical references and index.
    ISBN 1-56024-306-6 (alk. paper)
    1. AIDS (Disease)–Europe–Prevention. 2. Men–Europe–Sexual behavior. 3. Gay men–Europe–Sexual behavior. I. Title.
RA644.A25P66   1993
614.5'993–dc20

                                                                   92-18354
                                                                         CIP

CONTENTS

List of Tables

ABOUT THE AUTHOR

Michael Pollak, PhD, (1948-1992) was Director of Research at the *Centre National de la Recherche Scientifique* in Paris. He studied sociology in Austria and Paris and taught at the University of Montréal. As a sociologist, his main concern was the memory and the preservation of the social identity of individuals faced with difficult situations such as those in a homosexual community facing the AIDS epidemic or those confronted with the threat of extermination in concentration camps. The author of articles on topics including economy and sociology in France and a comparison of the nuclear controversy in France and in Germany, he also wrote comprehensive biographies of such influential sociologists as Paul F. Lazarsfeld and Max Weber. Dr. Pollak died of AIDS-related causes on June 7, 1992.

Homage to Michael Pollak

Michael Pollak died June 7, 1992, at age 43. Many of you knew him through his studies in sexuality, homosexuality, and AIDS in particular. Michael's sociological work was built around two main themes in these areas:

- the history of social sciences, which was a permanent research subject, the topic of his dissertation, and the subject of his last works on the history of the Ford Foundation and European social sciences
- the analysis of social identity in extreme situations.

Michael underlined the close link between these two theoretical concerns. His project on the social sciences essentially concentrated on disciplines devoted to the interactions between individual identities and collective identities, i.e., behavioral sciences. Therefore, identity is at the heart of all of his sociological interrogations.

He also wrote about Vienna, his birthplace, a capital seized in the grip of intellectual and artistic ferment at the turn of the century. The subtitle of his book revealed the direction of his analysis: *Vienne 1900: Une identité blessée (Vienna 1900: A Wounded Identity)*.

Deeply scarred by the horrors of World War II, he realized the fact that barbarianism might be the sociological outcome of a certain technocratic order. In his best book, *L'expérience concentrationnaire: Essai sur le maintien de l'identité sociale (The Concentrative Experience: Essay on the Maintenance of Social Identity)*, the extreme experience of deported women was taken as revealing identity as an image of oneself, an image for oneself, and an image for others. In his introduction, he dedicated the book to the identity and memory of these concentration camp prisoners. According to Michael, the loss of identity was characterized by a disparity between the individual's definition of herself and the social opinions of others. His analyses showed how individuals thus stigmatized attempt to maintain or restore the permanence of their social being.

His studies on homosexual lifestyles and the social consequences of AIDS were naturally incorporated into this questioning of identity and the affirmation of oneself in difficult times. In 1982, after two decades of "sexual liberation," his first article on male homosexuality underlined the difficulties he had in liberating himself from exclusively heterosexual socialization. Most homosexuals remain subjected to a schizophrenic management of their lives because their greatest source of suffering is caused by the relatively large gap between affectivity and sexuality.

In studying the lifestyles of the homosexual community and in opposition to a certain sociological tradition that mistrusts the implication of the researcher in the subject of his study, he affirmed his homosexuality. This affirmation was to the benefit of all. His homosexual life, his ensuing HIV positive status and illness, as well as his wide knowledge of the gay community, gave him the power to transgress; he dared introduce into scientific work a specific sensitivity. He achieved the impossible–integrating the human factor into his sociological work in a community too often stigmatized by views of homosexuality as deviant, even perverted, in relation to the heterosexual norm. He also studied how AIDS became the scope of a human and scientific commitment.

He was the initiator of a vast system for social observation and research projects: annual investigations of the most widely subscribed homosexual magazine in France, surveys including non-readers, individual in-depth interviews with HIV positive and bisexual people, studies on the associations battling AIDS, and participation in the investigations on the behavior and opinions of the general public regarding AIDS. Through this research system, which was unique in the world in its regularity and scope of investigations, Michael piloted quality research in the service of a cause which, beyond the tragedy of AIDS, affirmed homosexual identity. As rigorously as possible, he testified to the urgency of situations, while avoiding the dangers of cold scientific "neutrality" and the temptation of pity.

The quality of his sociological work has awakened wide interest in France as well as in the international scientific milieu. The European Community entrusted him with a comparative study on the politics of health and prevention and on the state of university research in 17 European countries. Upon completion of this project, he took responsibility in 1991 for a European survey using the French questionnaire as a model.

With his death we are deprived not only of the experience and competence of a sociologist, but also the warm presence of a vigilant man for whom an exact knowledge of homosexual lifestyles and the social consequences of AIDS was the best way to avert the exclusion that still victimizes homosexuals. He was highly conscious that the epidemic risked reinforcing a system of exclusion and discrimination–a system that Michael's permanent engagements led him to battle.

Marie-Ange Schiltz
Centre National de la Recherche Scientifique, Paris
Translated by Miriam Rabinovitch

Acknowledgments

When the importance of the epidemic was finally recognized in the political arena in 1989, the European Community established a Concerted Action with the aim of assessing AIDS prevention in the member countries. This Concerted Action intensified European cooperation in this field.

This Concerted Action was coordinated by the Institute of Social and Preventive Medicine in Lausanne, Switzerland with Fred Paccaud and Françoise Dubois-Arber as principal investigators. I was charged to study prevention activities in the field of men having sex with men. For the data collection I set up a network of country correspondents. Given the political changes on the European continent, I also invited representatives from the ex-German Democratic Republic, Czechoslovakia, and Poland. In two meetings in Paris a questionnaire was finalized and completed by the correspondents with the help of colleagues and administrators in their respective countries.

These correspondents did a magnificent job. Without their help, this book could not have been written:

- Austria: Wolfgang Dür
- Belgium: Michel Vincineau
- Canada: Michel Perrault
- Czechoslovakia: Richard Prusa
- Denmark: Jan Fouchard
- Federal Republic of Germany: Michael Bochow
- Finland: Olli Stalström
- German Democratic Republic: Rainer Herrn
- Great Britain: Peter Davies
- Greece: Gregory Vallianatos
- Ireland: Charles Kerrigan
- Italy: Francesco Allegrini, Hartmut Sasse
- Netherlands: Rob Tielman
- Norway: Annick Prieur

- Poland: Grzegorz Marian Okrent
- Spain: Oscar Guasch Andreu
- Sweden: Benny Henriksson
- Switzerland: Jean Blaise Masur

In identifying and selecting country correspondents for our group, some activist organizations were most helpful. Most of the members of our network are social scientists, some of whom have a medical background. Many have actively participated in voluntary AIDS work and/or are responsible for past and ongoing research and evaluation in this field. Most are self-identifying gay men or lesbians; some are self-identifying heterosexuals.

Clearly, sexual preference is a pre-condition neither for an ability to analyze gay organizations and behavior, nor for being allowed to do so. There is no specific "passport" for entering this field of study. Nevertheless, it would be naive to dismiss this question encountered in many investigations of minority groups: does being an "insider" or an "outsider" play a significant role in the choice of methodological and theoretical instruments and in the interpretation of data? Does it facilitate access (Bourdieu, 1980)? These questions should not be discussed abstractly. It was the scientific (medical) discourse of the nineteenth century that defined homosexuality as a sexual pathology, a mental disease or disorder. By doing so, it shaped discriminatory public attitudes and opinions, legislation and specific forms of exclusion which have lasted for decades. Only in the late 1960s did the liberalizing tendencies gain impetus. But residual inequalities under the law still exist in many countries, ranging from the age of sexual consent, indecency rules, and censorship of sexually explicit material to the prohibition of gay organizations identified as promotion agencies for homosexuality (ILGA, 1988). By definition, mentalities change slowly. For these reasons our group explicitly opted in favor of a position of solidarity with the gay movement. The struggle against AIDS has proved the importance of collective action, of community self-organization and self empowerment for fighting HIV transmission and social discrimination. Research can and should reinforce these tendencies. There is no contradiction between this ethical position and scientific rigor.

Michael Pollack

Introduction

This book is an enlarged and updated version of a collective effort to assess AIDS prevention in Western Europe. This effort was organized in the framework of a Concerted Action of the European Community. In addition to a group working on men having sex with men, other groups analyzed the general population, migrants and intravenous drug users (IVDUs).

The concentrated diffusion of HIV infection in a few marginalized groups creates specific problems for prevention, health information, education, and evaluation. From the beginning, prevention has had to face the difficult shaping of its messages: How to rapidly alert the most exposed groups and to bring about behavior changes without at the same time mobilizing medically unjustified panic reactions? How to formulate messages clearly addressed to fringe groups without stigmatizing them?

Although the proportion of homo- and bisexual men shows a decreasing tendency in AIDS surveillance statistics, they remain the most affected group. These figures become even more tragic if derived from the estimated proportion of gay men in the West European population. As a group particularly affected by the epidemic, male homo- and bisexuals reacted quickly by establishing their own prevention strategies. This capacity for early reaction also appeared in areas of scientific research relating to prevention. This reaction was favored, at least in some big cities (London, Paris, Berlin, Amsterdam, Copenhagen), by past experiences of sexually transmitted diseases (STDs) and hepatitis B which also affected promiscuous gay men in significant proportions. Some VD clinics had an established gay clientele. These relationships and the specific awareness of the medical personnel working in these centers has often functioned as a system of "first alert."

For obvious reasons, our report will document and emphasize this capacity for self-organization and self-help, an example of active solidarity. In our case, prevention has not followed a top-down information diffusion and education model. We will approach prevention as an example of social mobilization for fighting the transmission of a deadly disease. Therefore it is extremely difficult, as we will see, to attribute attitude and behavior changes to specific single factors or campaigns. These modifications, periodically documented by surveys, measure the synergy of a wide range of actions and interventions, designed and implemented by different actors using convergent and sometimes contradictory arguments.

OBJECTIVES

To collect and to compare existing information on:

1. The actors of prevention, community-based as well as public authorities; the formal and informal relationships between them, their complementarity and/or opposition.

2. The policies and major arguments used by these actors, as well as the settings chosen for targeted campaigns.

3. Studies conducted (with or without evaluative aims) among gay men using indicators such as life style, knowledge, attitudes, beliefs concerning HIV infection and AIDS, and measuring sexual practices and their modification as a response to the risk of HIV transmission.

4. Evaluation studies linked to identifiable campaigns and actions (e.g., hotlines, circulation of leaflets, etc.).

5. Data on the prevalence of HIV infection and AIDS concerning male homo- and bisexuals.

6. The risks (real, presumed, observed) of stigmatization of the group by the population in general, authorities, institutions, etc.

To proceed with a secondary analysis of the data collected in an attempt to answer the following questions:

1. Are the prevention policies in different European countries comparable? What are the convergencies and divergencies in terms of organization, actors involved, instruments used?

2. What are the principal problems encountered in campaigns, the limits and deficiencies observed? Whom do the campaigns really reach? How to access adolescents, men having sex with men but not identifying with a gay life style? What about male prostitution, from the point of view of sex workers as well as their clients? Do reactions of social stigmatization against homosexuals exist or, on the contrary, are there reactions of solidarity and group cohesion?

3. Are there indications that AIDS prevention programs had an effect on behavior? Can such changes be observed in all European countries or only in some? If differences exist, to what may one attribute them? Are there any arguments in favor of a causal relationship between prevention efforts and observed changes in behavior? What are the main problems mentioned by the people studied concerning the acquisition of protective behavior, and inversely what elements favor the acquisition and maintenance of protective behavior?

4. What are the research methodologies used: sampling, quantitative surveys, ethnographic studies, qualitative studies using in-depth interviewing and life histories? Do these different approaches address the problems of representativeness, reliability and validity of data? What are the methodologies best suitable for studying living conditions, sexuality, and protective behavior among gay men?

SOME LIMITS OF THIS STUDY

Population Size

The first problem encountered in this study is the difficulty of assessing the real size of the male population having sex with men. We have to rely on partial estimates based on self-reported behavior. These estimates depend on the definitions of the group of men having sex with men: Should one only include men who identify themselves as gay? Should one include married men who occasionally have sex with men, or all those who had at least one such experience? What about men dreaming about other men when they engage in solitary masturbation? These problems are common to all studies on sex and sexuality. In 1948, Kinsey estimated that just under 40% of the male population under study had at least some overt sexual experience to the point of orgasm with another man. Project SIGMA (Socio-sexual Investigations into Gay Men and AIDS) has shown that 60% of people identified as gay have had sex with a woman at some time. This shows the importance of bisexuality as a transient phenomenon. Most estimates and surveys concerning the sexual experience throughout life come to a 3-4% range of men having sex mainly with men (Fay et al., 1989). These figures might suffer from biases; some people will never disclose their sexual preference, and there is reason to believe that this is the case with people with low socio-cultural status even more than in the middle classes. In all surveys conducted in the general population the proportion of men having sex with men is significantly lower on the bottom of the social hierarchy.

Age Limits

The second difficulty is the age of consent (15 or 16 years in the Scandinavian countries, the Netherlands, Italy and Spain, 20 or 21 years in Switzerland and the United Kingdom, with other countries somewhere in between). These age limits have direct consequences for prevention as they restrict free discussion and presentation in schools of same-gender sexual activities. Also, in most countries, research which deals with sexual matters requires special authorizations from school administrations and parents to include adolescents. Therefore, very little, if anything, is known about gays in this age group. The considerable underrepresentation of the older generation (50+) in all surveys, irrespective of countries, occurs for different reasons. Only after the liberalization of the 1970s did homo- and bisexual men feel free to identify themselves as such. Social fears and hiding are still widespread in the older generation, making them more difficult to access. One can also add a feeling of exclusion in a commercial gay subculture which stresses youth and esthetic values.

Ethnic Minorities

For similar reasons, ethnic minorities and migrant workers having sex with men are difficult to reach in prevention and underrepresented in research. For cultural reasons, they seldom identify as "homosexuals." In Mediterranean countries only the partner being penetrated, not the one who penetrates, is labelled "homosexual" (Day, 1990). This has important ramifications for the comprehension of prevention materials and survey questions. These difficulties are exacerbated by the diversity of languages involved: Arabic, Turkish, Greek, Serbo-Croatic, etc.

Social Class and Geography

Finally, one observes a significant underrepresentation of people with low socioeconomic status and/or living outside urban centers. This underrepresentation could be explained in part by specific patterns of social and geographic mobility by which gays try to escape from hostile environments and find social niches more favorable to the realization of their desires (Dannecker and Reiche, 1974; Coxon, Davies, and McManus, 1990). This hypothesis, convincing as it is, explains only a small part of this underrepresentation. Rarely do research samples of male homo- and bisexuals include more than 5 to 7% of industrial blue collar workers.

These limitations of our study highlight the very real problems of accessing men having sex with men, a problem very difficult to overcome in prevention strategies as well as in research and evaluation. Therefore, the difficulties encountered in research always point to similar problems in prevention (Pollak, 1988a).

To answer the questions put forward above, our assessment exercise is twofold, partly based on original research materials, partly on secondary analysis. The first part of this report comparatively evaluates the epidemiological situation, as well as the policy context that has shaped approaches to prevention: organizational preconditions and frameworks, chronological landmarks, and the actors involved. The second part discusses the instruments of prevention, as well as the major arguments and images that have been used. For these two sections, the country correspondents provided original research materials that were complemented through country visits by the principal investigator. The third part is a secondary analysis of evaluation research and studies already published on the national level.

THE ORGANIZATION OF THE BOOK

The book is organized into three major parts. In the first, the context of prevention and its instruments are discussed. In the second, we analyze methodologies of assessment research undertaken in Western Europe and their result in terms of behavior change. In the third concluding part of the book, we will discuss successes and failures of prevention as shown by an analysis of epidemiological data. We then discuss the inadequacy of the Health Belief Model, which remains a major reference in the field of prevention.

Part One:
Organizing the Fight Against AIDS

THE CONTEXT OF PREVENTION

In several European countries, the first cases of AIDS were diagnosed only a few months after the first description of the syndrome in the CDC Morbidity and Mortality Weekly Report (1981). As in the United States, almost all cases diagnosed in the very first years of the epidemic were men in their thirties having sex with men. Despite the lessons from the United States, where a rapid increase in cases pointed to the epidemic nature of the phenomenon, the sociopolitical recognition of AIDS as a public health priority often took many years. Almost everywhere, voluntary associations preceded public authorities in organizing prevention and in building alliances with medical networks. Gay organizations played a major role in this phase. Often public authorities had difficulties finding the appropriate way of entering into communication with male homo- and bisexuals, and so they used gay organizations as intermediaries. In Vienna, Austria, the first prevention leaflet was distributed by the Homosexual Initiative (HOSI) as early as 1983 when the first cases were diagnosed. This project was financed by the health authorities of the city government. The same model was later implemented at the state level, with the chancellor's office responsible for general campaigns and the Österreichische (Austrian) AIDS Hilfe (ÖAH) for targeted approaches. The same organizational division of labor between governmental bodies and non-governmental organizations (NGOs) emerged in many European countries.

The strength of preventive approaches in medical traditions also shaped the early response to the epidemic. As in STD and, some decades ago, tuberculosis prevention, there exists a clear gap between Northern and Southern Europe in AIDS prevention. The

Scandinavian countries, the United Kingdom, and the Netherlands were much quicker in implementing preventive strategies than the Mediterranean South. Germany, France, Austria, and Switzerland occupy an intermediate position. As we will see, these medical traditions and organizational conditions are more important explanatory elements than the state of the epidemic itself.

Legal restrictions on condom promotion and sales were lifted in France in 1987, but they still exist in Ireland where condoms are sold exclusively to persons over 18 years, and only in drugstores and family planning clinics. In East European countries, the major problem is production, distribution, and quality of condoms. This has been clearly demonstrated in a Soviet presentation at the Seventh International Conference on AIDS. Although gay men do not represent the most dominant group, they represent 40 percent of cases. In a survey of 400 gay men, 71 percent indicated that they have never used a condom (Pokrovsky and Eramova, 1991).

Moralistic attitudes and religious organizations are another element hindering prevention through the condemnation of homosexual relationships as well as, in the case of the Catholic Church, the prohibition of condoms. Homophobic attitudes have delayed or made impossible targeted information campaigns in several countries, in particular the Mediterranean countries and Ireland. As in other areas, such as divorce, abortion, and sex education in school, churches have a lobbying power irrespective of public opinion, including that of their own membership, which often favors more liberal solutions (Tielman and de Jonge, 1988).

In Poland, the increasing church influence on political life will probably have adverse effects on prevention in the male homo- and bisexual population. Strong homophobic attitudes still persist in Czechoslovakia, in public attitudes and legal provisions. Organizational relationships have been established between these countries and NGOs in neighboring countries. The Austrian AIDS Hilfe (ÖAH) has privileged relationships with Czech, Slovak, and Hungarian organizations. The German AIDS Hilfe was helpful in establishing and in helping its eastern counterparts before and after the unification of the country.

CHRONOLOGICAL LANDMARKS
AND ORGANIZATIONAL CONDITIONS

The delay between the first diagnosed AIDS cases, the first action organized by voluntary associations and, later, by public agencies, range from a few months to several years (Table 1). Only in Finland, Norway, Sweden, and the Netherlands did public authorities organize prevention in a proactive way before or in the same year as the appearance of the first AIDS cases in the country.

In addition to strong traditions of preventive and social medicine, specific organizational preconditions and social mobilizations account for these differences. The following were preconditions for the emergence and stabilization of community-based AIDS work (Perrow and Guillen, 1990):

- the recognition of AIDS as a major problem in the concerned communities;
- the existence of community-based networks that can be mobilized;
- the possibility of alliance building;
- financial resources.

In Europe the first two conditions were closely related. The stronger and better-organized the gay community and the less the social fears concerning stigmatization, the earlier AIDS was identified as a major health problem affecting gays. Organizing and alliance building around the AIDS issue could then take place very rapidly. In countries where gay organizations are weak, fragile and/or fragmented, ambivalent attitudes prevailed among male homo- and bisexuals and in the gay press. Was AIDS just another instrument for reversing liberalizing trends and sexual emancipation or a very real health problem concerning gay men even more than others? In most countries where an organized gay community hardly exists, the first of these interpretations prevailed in the gay press before 1984/85, the second–AIDS as a gay health issue–became dominant thereafter. Lack of self-confidence, defensive attitudes such as counter-accusations, denial, or reluctance are major factors for late prevention. Despite their almost exclusive gay constituency, AIDS organizations do not necessarily define themselves as gay organizations.

TABLE 1. Chronological landmarks.

Authorities	Year of first AIDS diagnosis	First prevention action NGOs	First prevention action Public
Austria	1983	1983	1986
Belgium	<1981	1985	1985
Denmark	<1981	1984	1984
Finland	1982	1982	1986
France	<1981	1985	1987
Germany F.R.	1981	1983	1985
Greece	1984	—	1985
Ireland	1982	1986	1986
Italy	1982	1984	1989
Netherlands	1982	1982	1983
Norway	1983	1983	1985
Portugal	1983	—	1986
Spain	<1981	1983	1985
Sweden	1982	1981	1985
Switzerland	<1981	1984	1986
United Kingdom	<1981	1982	1986

Source: WHO collaborating center on AIDS, country correspondents. The dates for "first prevention action" refer to prevention in the general and/or in the male homo-bisexual population. Often prevention started with educational programs addressed to the medical personnel to limit fear reactions in hospitals.

Some even explicitly reject such labels. AIDES in France and AIDS-Hilfe in Austria are cases in point. Where representatives of gay organizations could play the role of community spokesmen, they were able to negotiate policies and programs with public authorities. But as importantly, they were able to enroll gay business in the prevention effort. In the absence of such organizations, self-help structures appeared much later, between 1984 and 1986. Even government reactions were slower, primarily due to the lack of social pressure put on decision makers.

It is now possible to produce a schematic typology-and-country profile in the field of AIDS prevention. Table 2 presents the conditions for the rapid emergence of self-help organizations.

Table 3 shows in field 1 the ability of well-organized gay organizations to convert themselves to AIDS work or to add it to their traditional preoccupations. Here gay militancy and community organizations have been able to undergo a rapid reorientation. A few years later (1984 and 1985) strong AIDS organizations emerged in Germany, Switzerland, Austria, and France, playing a catalyzing and coordinating role (field 3). Most volunteers in these organizations are gay men and an important proportion of them HIV+ (although we do not pretend to quantify this phenomenon). Here, the major criterion for organizing was proximity to the disease. Conversions of gay activists were rare in comparison to the involvement of volunteers with no activist past. In this specific context, Daniel Defert, president of French AIDES, is right to speak about the "patient as a social reformer" (Defert, 1990). Field 4 represents countries where AIDS organizations not identified as gay organizations have remained fragmented regionally and/or on ideological grounds. Field 6 is very similar, but some organizations in these countries do identify with a gay community.

Two countries do not appear on this chart. In fact, one hardly can speak about AIDS organizations (gay or not) in Greece and Portugal. The social climate and self-definitions that cause men having sex with men to avoid group identification are not conducive to organized work. Under pressure of the AIDS issue, a voluntary gay organization has been created in the northern part of Portugal. For social reasons its initiators preferred not to register it officially. In

TABLE 2. Organizational strength of gay organizations and of preventive medicine.

	High	Low
High	1) Norway, Sweden, Finland, Denmark, Netherlands	2) Germany F.R., Switzerland, Austria, Belgium, United Kingdom
Low	3)	4) France, Italy, Spain, Ireland Greece, Portugal

TABLE 3. The field of voluntary AIDS associations.

	Highly coordinated ("Umbrella organizations")	Fragmented
Explicitly gay based	1) Scandinavian countries (Norway, Finland, Denmark), Netherlands	2)
Not explicitly gay based	3) Germany F.R., Switzerland, Austria, France (before 1988)	4) Spain
Both	5) Germany F.R. (after 1987)	6) United Kingdom, France (after 1988), Italy, Belgium

both countries some gay men do important lobbying work, on an individual level on discrimination issues.

COUNTRY PROFILES

In the Scandinavian countries and the Netherlands reactions have been channelled through gay and lesbian organizations. Most of these national organizations have longstanding traditions, as they come out of the sexual reform movement of the 1940s and 1950s (Netherlands: COC: 1946; Denmark: LBL: 1948; Sweden: RFSL: 1950; Norway: DNF: 1950, FHO: 1980). Finland joined this group much later when, in 1974, SETA, an organization of sexual equality, was created (with technical help and advice by the Dutch COC and the Swedish RFSL). The strategy of these organizations can be described as one of social integration and negotiation with public authorities. Most of these umbrella organizations have a few thousand members, organize a few hundred volunteers, and are managed by a limited number of full-time professionals. Their high organizational cohesion and social recognition has allowed them to quickly define AIDS as a health issue which particularly concerns men with homosexual contacts.

Gay-based foundations for health and psychological advice, established in these countries in the 1960s and 1970s, have reoriented part of their work towards AIDS activities. With the help of these gay umbrella organizations, AIDS self-help associations servicing all parts of society and all infected people have been established, such as the Finnish AIDS Information and Support Center and the Norwegian Gay and Lesbian Health Committee. Groups of gay doctors formed, such as a community health center in Amsterdam. In the Welfare State tradition, almost 90 to 100 percent of their resources come from public funding.

In these same North European countries, traditions of preventive medicine and epidemiological surveillance are well established, and so medical authorities also relatively quickly organized their intervention programs. According to national traditions, however, these interventions took quite different forms.

In Holland, actions of NGOs and public authorities are closely coordinated: gay representatives (three official representatives of gay organizations and two openly gay men) sit on the National Committee on AIDS Control, first established in 1983. Altogether five out of 25 members are gay. The government usually follows this committee's advice, given its broad professional background. As a result, the Dutch approach is very liberal, based on information, education, and persuasion. The important gay representation in decision making also explains the weight given to discrimination and stigmatization issues.

In contrast to the Netherlands, the Swedish and Finnish AIDS state committees and advisory commissions (created in 1984 and 1985) were rather medically dominated with no gay representatives. Intensive contacts between health services and gay organizations exist at the regional and local level. In both countries, HIV was defined legally as a venereal disease. This opened the avenue for state intervention including the closing of gay saunas, anonymous registration and surveillance of HIV+ people, compulsory partner-tracing programs and, in Sweden, the possibility of isolation of HIV carriers in case of noncompliance. This administrative approach reflects the tradition of preventive medicine as a means of social control. Only Bavaria comes close to this catalogue of coercive measures. The Swedish government's response to the epidemic fuelled conflict and controversy in 1985. Gay organizations felt that their important work was totally neglected and being destroyed. It took months to restore some confidence and to reestablish more cooperative relationships (Henriksson, 1988; Direction Nationale de la Santé et Affaires Sociales, 1988).

Norway and Denmark lie between these two extreme cases of liberal Holland and coercive Sweden. Partner-tracing programs are conducted on a voluntary basis. Some openly gay men sit on government advisory boards.

In the next group of countries–the Federal Republic of Germany, Switzerland and Austria, a gay organizational infrastructure hardly existed. The first initiatives for building self-help organizations came from concerned individuals, mostly gay, often HIV+. But seldom did they have any past experience of gay militancy. Clearly, they defined their action as a general and global response to the AIDS crisis, including targeted prevention and education efforts, self-help for seropositives and people with AIDS, as well as their family members. They quickly mobilized hundreds of volunteers and built alliances with health officials and concerned doctors. With the noticeable exception of Bavaria, this has reduced coercion and facilitated a liberal and open approach toward AIDS. In comparison with their Austrian and Swiss counterparts, the Deutsche AIDS-Hilfe has been more explicit and outspoken on gay issues. Financed almost exclusively by public subsidies, these AIDS umbrella organizations employ a comparatively high number of permanent paid staff: in former West Germany: 40 on the federal level, 300 in the regional organizations; in Switzerland: 10 full-time positions on the federal and 25 on the regional level–with the opening of regional offices, this last figure will increase in the coming years; in Austria: 100 nationwide, one-third on a full-, two-thirds on a part-time basis. This organizational structure, on almost 100 percent public financial support, transforms these AIDS-Hilfen into quasi-public administrations. The most dense network is found in West Germany.

After a period of intensive, often radical forms of gay militancy in the style of the "sixties" movement, it almost collapsed in the early 1980s in the United Kingdom and France. There was no continuity on which to build AIDS organizations. As the European country culturally closest to the United States, Britain's gay media soon took the AIDS issue very seriously and mobilized with the Lesbian and Gay Medical Association, created in 1982. In the United Kingdom, concerned people created the Terrence Higgins Trust in 1982, which today employs some 30 full-time salaried staff and organizes 1000 volunteers. With sympathetic support by the Terrence Higgins Trust, ethnic groups (black, Asians) were organized in 1989.

As in the United Kingdom, the French organization AIDES, created in late 1984, became operational in 1985. It is mainly run by gay men (Hirsch, 1991). Altogether, several hundred volunteers work in 30 regional committees. Despite the regional structure of AIDES, which is in competition with hundreds of small local organizations, the network density in France is relatively weak. In France, too, there is hardly any continuity between the gay militancy of the 1970s and AIDS organizers. In both countries the major AIDS organizations (Terrence Higgins Trust and AIDES) define themselves as general interest groups with responsibility for organizing prevention and support for people with AIDS and for maintaining a positive social climate for the infected. Nevertheless, their constituency remains largely gay. The share of female volunteers in AIDES has increased from only 5 percent in the beginning to 30 percent of new members in 1989, but has since dropped. As in the United Kingdom, public subsidies account for only 30-40 percent of these organizations' overall budgets. They must devote major efforts to fund raising. Usually, fund-raising activities are combined with promotion of prevention. An important proportion of these activities takes place in the gay community. Group solidarity has become an important element for the growth of these organizations and the services they offer. Government response to and recognition of these efforts differs greatly in these two countries. After organizing a first TV information campaign in 1987, the French government has finally recognized the importance of the AIDS problem through the creation, in 1989, of three agencies with substantial financial resources: one responsible for AIDS research (including social sciences), another for prevention, and a National Council dealing with a wide range of ethical issues. Not until late 1986 did the British government become involved in AIDS prevention through the regional health authorities which formed health education teams. The National Health Education Authority established a special division for AIDS, but this administration is presently under reorganization and there will no longer be a specific AIDS division. The signs are that the future will bring diminished public support and a growing climate of adversarial government approaches, particularly when gay issues are involved.

In Italy and Spain, where no single organization has gained a dominant position in this field, diversity prevails among a few large organizations based in the major cities or regions. In Spain the period of transition from Francoism to democracy has favored the blossoming of gay commercial establishments (Guasch Andreu, 1987), but activist organizations are of a rather ephemeral type. Organized nationally with its seat in Bologna, the most important Italian gay organization, Arci Gay, devotes a significant proportion of its work to HIV prevention (Moss, 1990). In both countries, regional autonomy has shaped organizational diversity. Only recent coordination has given rise to national non-gay voluntary associations, League for the Struggle Against AIDS (LILA) in Italy (1987), and the Federation of Citizen Commissions against AIDS in Spain (1987), which claims several hundreds of volunteers all over the country and employs some 25 people as permanent staff. In Italy and Spain these organizations receive no significant public financial support. Rather, local and regional authorities offer some technical assistance, office space, and free telephone lines. In Belgium, the situation is complicated by the division of the country into two linguistic communities that form separate regional administrative units. For a long time AIDS has been perceived as a problem of foreign labor or of Africans coming for treatment to Belgium. Only after 1985 did the government become concerned with prevention (Hubert, 1990). At the same time voluntary associations, gay-based and not, formed. Most of them are small, with two to four permanent staff and a few dozen volunteers per association. Traditional NGOs, such as "Social Services for Foreigners," Third World doctors, and Family Planning also entered the field. Public subsidies represent up to 60 percent of the financing of associations, but many have no public support at all.

Despite important individual involvement, NGOs play a limited role in Greece and Portugal. The Greek "National Committee for AIDS," composed of university professors and church representatives, has a limited epidemiological and biomedical perspective. In Portugal, the "National Committee against AIDS" comprises five members from the significant departments of the Ministry of Health. Television campaigns first started in 1987. Emphasis is on education of professionals, with the help of charitable organizations (church-based). No specific campaigns directed toward men having sex with men have been designed.

With a few exceptions, AIDS organizations in most European countries have not yet reached the financial and organizational level which would allow them to engage in a long-term employment policy enabling them to professionalize their services. Most of their staff is recruited on the basis of national government-backed employment schemes or of objectors to military conscription choosing the alternative social services.

INTERNATIONAL NETWORKING

Early recognition and AIDS-mobilization have been favored by existing or newly established networks. In the early stages, the gay press played an important role as a disseminator of news from the United States. The United Kingdom and Ireland benefitted from their linguistic advantage. Despite the fragility of gay organizations in these countries, mobilization took place very early. In other countries a cautious line persisted in gay newspapers until 1984.

Most European AIDS organizations have some relationships among themselves and with their American counterparts, the New York-based Gay Men's Health Crisis and the San Francisco-based Shanti project being the most important contacts. Inside Europe, geographic and linguistic factors shape the intensity of contacts. Scandinavian and Dutch AIDS organizations, gay-based or not, have continuous contacts and working relationships. Their affiliation to the International Lesbian and Gay Organization (ILGA) plays an important role. The German, Austrian and Swiss AIDS-Hilfe are also closely interrelated, exchanging materials, posters and information. The French-speaking parts of Switzerland and Belgium have privileged relationships with the French organization AIDES, which also cooperates closely with Greek,

Spanish and Portuguese AIDS activists on an individual and, where possible, an organizational level. For obvious reasons Irish organizations have privileged relationships with the Terrence Higgins Trust.

Under the auspices of the World Health Organization (WHO), more formal coordination efforts resulted in the first international AIDS Service Organizations Conference that took place in Vienna in 1989, followed by a second conference a few months later. These conferences gave rise to the European Council of AIDS Service Organizations. At present, a WHO-supported international comparative project is assessing the financial, organizational and recruitment patterns of NGOs. This project is coordinated by the Vienna-based European Center for Social Welfare, Training and Research. Also in Vienna, ILGA organized AIDS workshops at its 1989 Conference.

These coordination efforts now also include the Eastern countries, represented at the first European Conference on HIV and Homosexuality, organized in Copenhagen in early 1990. This international network enables organizations to exchange experiences, to learn from each other, and to adapt foreign materials to their own style and context. It has specific importance for countries starting AIDS work and where voluntary associations are weak and fragile.

PRESENT TRENDS

In most countries, NGOs have preceded actions by public authorities, but when governments commissioned large newspaper and TV campaigns from communication agencies, voluntary associations often felt marginalized or excluded, a feeling exacerbated by the absence of any reference, in those campaigns, to the practices of men having sex with men. As early as 1985, such tensions emerged in Sweden at the moment of the first government information campaign. The same is true in France, where the creation of a government agency for prevention created some suspicion among voluntary organizations that the government would coordinate and dominate all AIDS work.

The field of AIDS organizations changed along with the epidemic. Self-help organizations have become more radical as hope for a rapid medical solution has vanished. Voluntary AIDS work that grew out of gay organizations had to adapt to a growing non-gay clientele. While AIDS organizations had once avoided a gay image, they found themselves increasingly neglecting this declining segment of the AIDS population. Gay self-help groups which emerged in France in the late 1980s created pressure inside AIDES to establish a specific gay group for prevention. Finally, more and more seropositives and people with AIDS undergo a "coming out" process as HIV-infected people. Their place is of increasing importance inside traditional AIDS organizations and in a new more radical generation, such as the British and Irish Body Positive Groups, Act Up, and similar organizations in France and Spain.

In the German-speaking countries, with their large umbrella organizations, rapid organizational and financial growth and personnel decisions concerning permanent salaried staff have given impetus to conflict over efficiency criteria and the real influence of the volunteers over strategic decisions. These organizational tensions are exacerbated by the rapid turnover of volunteers and the burnout problem that emerges in AIDS organizations, as it does in hospital services in big cities where the gay population is severely affected. The experience of dying and grief adds to this depressing picture.

Only two studies have analyzed these problems. In France, an evaluation project, financed by the Ministry of Social Affairs, has been conducted on two NGOs: AIDES and APARTS. In the Netherlands, the Schorerstichting, a gay service organization, undertook an audit study for evaluating its points of tension (Pollak and Rosman, 1989; de Rijk and van den Boom, 1989). According to the demands of its clients, the Schorerstichting had to increase the share of its AIDS work from 20 percent a few years ago to almost 80 percent. The French and the Dutch evaluation studies show an extremely rapid turnover rate of volunteers. Many volunteers stay only a few months in AIDS work. Only a few persist longer than two years. Salaried staff is submitted to extreme stress created by the permanent feeling of urgency.

In a 1990 evaluation, the work of the Swiss AIDS-Hilfe was very positively perceived, though tensions were observed between the two major factions: male homosexuals and women. These tensions can be partly explained by rapid growth and the lack of time to adapt to a changing environment, and by accusations concerning an overrepresentation of gay men in the directing bodies. The evaluation study concludes that this representation has never been more than 30 percent of voting members, corresponding to their work load and importance.

Large NGOs have entered the field of AIDS work, including prevention; the Red Cross occupies an important position in Sweden, Spain, and Ireland, while Family Planning organizations presently engage in AIDS work in several countries, as do Church-based social services, such as Caritas in Austria, and others in Southern Germany and Portugal. This organizational diversification results in competition for scarce resources.

After almost ten years of the epidemic, these developments indicate that AIDS work has arrived at a turning point: the diversity of actors involved, the renegotiation of alliances and of the appropriate areas of intervention for private versus public, for gay-based versus general actors.

Gay organizations call this development "degaying of AIDS," accusing public authorities of holding flattering lipservices to the gay community's exemplary actions while at the same time tending to exclude them from decision making. Significantly, the title of the first European Conference on AIDS and Homosexuality in early 1990 was: "Regaying AIDS."

In this context, our own assessment of policy contexts clearly shows the importance of the following factors:

- Rapid recognition of AIDS as a major health problem depends on the existence of a (gay) network able to mobilize the concerned communities.
- Alliance building with parts of the medical community and health authorities is essential for organizing prevention in a favorable social climate.
- In the European context private philanthropy is limited. Public support is the condition for a long-lasting effort in this field.
- Gay-based associations are the main (if not the only) guarantee for accessing men having sex with men. In close cooperation with health authorities they can provide a multiplier effect and maximum efficiency at limited costs.

• International networks can help early recognition and mobilization on the national level. They can provide organizational help and facilitate reciprocal learning.

PREVENTION INSTRUMENTS

Information

As raising individual responsibility is the declared objective of AIDS prevention in all European countries, information and education have become primary concerns. A wide range of informational materials are used in all European countries, from leaflets and handbooks to street advertisements and TV spots. According to organizational frameworks and the relationships between voluntary associations and public authorities, the first printed materials were conceived and distributed by NGOs. With the choice of more cost intensive media, such as TV and street advertisements, public authorities entered the field, independently or in close cooperation with existing NGOs. Communication specialists and advertisement agencies also became powerful partners.

Obviously, men having sex with men are part of the general population. Therefore it would be absurd to oppose information campaigns directed toward the whole population or specifically conceived for men having sex with men. In the discussion about the respective efficiency of general versus targeted efforts, one has to distinguish between the problems of accessing different segments of the population and the question of the appropriate messages for each segment: How to reach as high a proportion as possible of men having sex with men? How to provide them with all the information they need for modifying their sexual practices to avoid the risk of HIV transmission? These questions have to be considered separately.

In the early days of the epidemic, voluntary associations (explicitly gay or not), which distributed informational materials, "targeted" men having sex with men even if the messages about the methods of transmission did not specifically address homosexual practices. The leaflets and posters of those days allow us to trace the history of the development of a specific prevention language. This language avoids stigmatizing terms such as the "risk group" concept. It has banned value judgments concerning sexual choices, preferences, or type of partners. It concentrates on practices that favor HIV transmission and addresses the question of how to protect against it. At the same time, informational materials have to fight against exaggerated fears and misperceptions concerning transmission in everyday life situations (shaking hands, the use of public toilets, etc.), against stigmatization and discrimination. This elaboration has taken more or less time in different countries and provoked controversies about the degree of sexual explicitness and the importance given to condom promotion. Controversies refer not only to the language, but also to the illustrations in informational materials. When the messages moved from a logic of negative prohibition ("avoid . . . ," "don't . . .") to positive prescriptive attitudes, the concept of safer sex placed a high value on alternatives.

At the same time, new social demands for information and guidance required answers in prevention materials: under which circumstances should one take the test? How to live with the HIV infection, either with one's own infection or with infected relatives or friends? Here, the primary themes are solidarity and the refusal of social exclusion.

These two developments toward sexual explicitness, on the one hand, and on the other the introduction of the theme "How to live with it," reintroduced the debate on how to manage specific practices and groups. For safer sex, education materials are often specifically addressed to men having sex with men and use explicit illustrations. Even inside gay organizations, concerns were expressed about how such explicitness could affect the social image of the group. In Germany, negotiations with public authorities over subsidies raised the issue of the dividing line between AIDS information and pornography. When surveys tried to evaluate the acceptance of such materials among men having sex with men, the results were usually very positive. In Austria, an explicit condom comic of men having sex with men was very successful. In Germany, such explicit material distributed in gay meeting places ranged very high in perception and approval in a Knowledge, Attitude, Belief, and Practice Survey, and in France a questionnaire added to a safer sex leaflet for men having sex with men was answered by more than 1,000 respondents. It showed that gay men welcomed its explicitness and even wished for more detail in the illustrations (Pollak and Pelé et al., 1990). These reactions also underline the importance of humor that gives a positive value to changes in sexual practices.

Solidarity campaigns have developed along two major lines: testimonies by seropositives or people with AIDS, and public statements given by prominent people in arts, sports or politics. Public testimonies by seropositives signal an important turning point in the social management and the public perception of the epidemic. Such testimonies bring the realities of the suffering human being closer to people and transform AIDS from an abstract, far-away phenomenon into a concrete reality that people can identify with. Also, it might help people with AIDS to break the silence and to liberate themselves from the burden of a solitary fight. Nevertheless, such testimonies are extremely difficult to conceive and to manage, be it in newspapers or on TV. First of all, the people concerned must be ready to go public, to disclose their serostatus and/or their sexuality. One has also to take into consideration the potential negative effects reinforcing widespread prejudices on drug use and sexuality. Carefully prepared testimonies and solidarity campaigns have had positive effects in the overall population and the concerned groups.

As these themes and their importance are also closely linked to the state and the size of the epidemic, they are not equally developed in all countries. Also, when public authorities massively entered the field of information in street advertisement or on TV, they did not necessarily build their campaigns on the experiences cumulated by voluntary associations.

This report cannot give a complete analysis of informational materials diffused by associations and public authorities. It can only present a few dimensions of it, describe some characteristic country styles, and stress differences in the presentation of the methods of transmission.

In the Netherlands, Switzerland, Germany, Austria, and–more recently–France, associations and public authorities have, more or less successfully, developed a common prevention language and style. Almost from the beginning, the Dutch prevention materials were based on practices and highly technical information. Years before other countries, they stressed the importance of special condoms for anal penetration and the use of appropriate lubricants. Also, in the absence of such condoms, materials advised abstention from anal penetration. Elaborated in close collaboration, distributed by very diverse channels, the Dutch prevention work benefitted from the tradition of a liberal approach toward sexuality and homosexuality. "How to speak about it?"–this question seems to pose fewer problems here than in most other countries.

In Germany, Austria, and Switzerland, the public authorities have, to a large extent, delegated the production and diffusion of targeted materials to the respective AIDS-Hilfen. The early creation of local offices gave optimal efficiency to targeted strategies, as leaflet and poster distributions were not concentrated only in a few big cities. These materials stress the importance of condoms and the pursuit of a protected free sexuality, but also the importance of community belonging and participation in gay life in order to avoid self-isolation. The posters of the Deutsche AIDS-Hilfe, of very high aesthetic standards, have become collector's items, in Germany and elsewhere, entering into many sleeping rooms of gay men. In street advertisements and TV clips, used for consciousness-raising rather than for explicit sex information, gay images were not specifically developed.

The style of Austrian posters is very similar, but less diversified and less sexually explicit. As in Belgium, Italy, Norway, Spain, and Switzerland, love, tenderness and monogamy are mentioned as positive alternatives to an anonymous sex life. In Italy and Austria, the sense of family and pediatric cases played a prominent role in newspaper advertisements. In Switzerland, a common symbol and slogan have been developed, used by the AIDS-Hilfe and the federal and many cantonal administrations: a condom signed "Stop AIDS." Swiss campaigns also recommend monogamy as one alternative for protection.

In Ireland, where homosexuality is still not legal, voluntary associations have developed a very active strategy that links AIDS education with group self-empowerment. In most countries, AIDS information stresses individual responsibility for oneself and for one's sexual partners. The Irish activists have enlarged this concept of responsibility and speak about "community consciousness and responsibility." Their exemplary work develops in a hostile environment of social actors (administrations, the church, etc.) who insist rather on fear and abstinence, and where condoms have sometimes been presented as useless for anal sex.

In France, a very specific strategy has developed over the years. In the early stages of the disease, condom promotion was limited by law. The major association, AIDES, avoided speaking in terms of specific groups. Only after 1988 did the prevention administration, advised by several expert groups, develop a double strategy: give a positive value to safer sex and eroticize the condom without mentioning AIDS, along with solidarity campaigns for seropositives and people with AIDS (PWA).

Where little coordination exists between associations and public authorities, contradictory and sometimes conflicting arguments have emerged. In the United Kingdom, where the Terrence Higgins Trust and gay associations had argued in terms of condoms and safer sex, the government campaigns, only begun in 1986, were based on fear ("Don't die of ignorance"), giving no practical sexual guidance. In Sweden, the government campaign, first implemented in 1985, was an incentive for getting tested. The illustration in the newspaper ads showed situations considered at risk: a blonde Swedish girl on a southern beach meeting a boy with black hair, a young man in a train meeting a gay man presented in a stereotyped clone image. These advertisements combine suggestions for avoidance with incentives for the test. But they do not speak explicitly about safer sex. Perceived as stigmatizing and useless, they were attacked by gay associations. Danish, French, and Swiss materials also contain incentives for taking the test.

In several countries–Denmark, Finland, Germany, Great Britain, the Netherlands, Norway, Sweden and Quebec–there has been a move over the last two years towards integrating AIDS prevention into a more general STD prevention. Condom promotion is then represented more generally as a protection from all sorts of STDs.

Some differences still exist in the presentation of risk practices that favor HIV transmission. In Spanish comic-style TV clips, exchange of toothbrushes is considered risky. Uncertainties concerning oral sex are reflected in the different attitudes toward it. While West German materials give only the advice not to swallow semen, in France and Finland condoms are now systematically advised for oral sex. A Finnish AIDS Center safe sex brochure even suggests how to make condoms more acceptable in oral sex by using jelly or honey.

Health Education

Most remarks on information materials also apply to health education, though it is a broader approach than information, including more interactive elements. In most countries health authorities have organized special training sessions and weekend seminars on AIDS for health and social workers. They are organized on the local, hospital level, and sometimes on a larger scale by health administrations or the Red Cross. Medical aspects usually dominate such sessions, but the unique requirements of health work with marginalized and stigmatized groups has favored the introduction of psychological and social dimensions, often explicitly addressing the question of homo- and bisexual relationships.

For the gay community, volunteer training in AIDS organizations was a major instrument for reciprocal learning and for a wider diffusion of knowledge. The British Terrence Higgins Trust, the French AIDES, the German, Austrian, and Swiss AIDS-Hilfe, as well as their Dutch, Scandinavian, Italian, and Irish counterparts, developed similar training programs. They are organized in several evening sessions or on one or two weekends. Aside from the medical aspects, time is devoted to psychological and social dimensions. The pedagogical techniques include technical support, such as videoclips, interactive role playing, and learning how to express individual emotions and feelings.

One should not look at volunteer training in too limited a perspective. When people contact a voluntary association, biographical motifs can be complex and of paramount importance: mourning, learning one's own seropositivity, etc. In France, an evaluation study has shown that some 30 percent of people going through the volunteer training of AIDES finally decide not to become volunteers (Pollak and Rosman, 1989). But this high drop-out rate is no indication of failure. They all have received an intensive, high-quality AIDS education and can become disseminators of this message among their friends. For seropositives and people with AIDS, such training programs can improve their capacity to negotiate with their doctors.

Reinforcing Safer Sex Behavior

From volunteer training and the experience of infected people in self-help groups, safer sex workshops have developed, most of which are specifically designed for men having sex with men. First created in the United States and Australia, they now exist in many major cities in Western Europe. They are intended to reinforce safer sex attitudes and stabilize and maintain safe behaviors. They give a positive value to alternatives to risky sex and stress the erotic dimensions of such practices, including condoms. Organized in small groups, they are built on peer support concepts (Gordon, unpublished).

"Jack-off" clubs pursue the same objective, not through cognitive instruments, but through forms of practical learning. Group sex practices are very important to a significant minority of men having sex with men. AIDS educators sought ways to reach these men and to motivate them for safer sex practices. First organized in major American cities in the early 1980s, "Jack-off" clubs began to appear in 1987-1988 in Amsterdam, Paris, Marseille, Vienna (Austria) and a few large German cities. From one hundred to two hundred people usually come to the gatherings with strict rules. They take place in full light, often start with a short introduction explaining how to avoid HIV transmission and the rules of the games allowed in the club. Often condoms are distributed. Nevertheless, during the gatherings anal penetration, even with condoms, is prohibited. The practices performed are erotic massages and caresses as well as solitary and mutual masturbation. These gatherings are also perfect occasions for voyeurism and exhibitionism as positive alternatives to risk practices.

A first questionnaire evaluation study of the Paris "Jacks" was made in 1987, and a year later the same research team undertook a comparative study of the Paris and Amsterdam "Jacks" (Bergès, Pelé, and Pollak, 1988; Algra et al., 1989). In 1987, 425 questionnaires were distributed to all participants of these consecutive parties, 244 (57 percent) were returned. In 1988, 520 questionnaires were distributed in Paris, 412 in Amsterdam. The return was 275 (53 percent) in Paris, 169 (41 percent) in Amsterdam. The majority of participants come from a middle-class background, the average

age is 38 years. The major motives for participation are specific sexual pleasures (voyeurism), the feeling of group belonging, and the opportunity for learning new sexual conduct. Thirty-three percent of respondents in Paris and 20 percent in Amsterdam stated that the "Jack-off" parties helped them start to regularly practice safer sex. For HIV positive people, these parties are often the first occasion for resuming sexual activities. Also, 19 percent in Paris and 17 percent in Amsterdam discovered new sexual pleasures. The comparative survey reveals that the move toward safer sex started later in Paris than in Amsterdam. It also confirms different behavior patterns that reflect the prevention strategies in the two countries. Compared to France, Dutch gay men have drastically reduced all sexual activities except for mutual masturbation. This is especially true for anal intercourse and for oro-genital contacts. Significant differences also exist with regard to the test, which is favored in France and rather rejected in the Netherlands. In Amsterdam, 68 percent, versus 30 percent in Paris, are not tested. Among the tested respondents, 27 percent were seropositive in Paris, and 21 percent in Amsterdam.

In a time of constraint and crisis for a sexually very active group, "Jack-off" parties fulfill significant functions: they are conducive to safer sex and help stabilize new behavior, and they provide a safe place for the ritualized and collective sexual activities that many gay men seek.

Hot Lines

Hot lines are a major working instrument for almost all AIDS organizations, voluntary associations, and local and regional health services. As an information and education instrument, they offer the possibility for interaction and a personalized but anonymous counseling service. The callers' concerns also change as the epidemic develops. The experiences of hot line volunteers were instrumental in developing an ethic of listening and non-judgmental attitudes. They also demonstrated how important sexual explicitness is for AIDS-prevention work.

Most hot line services are offered to the general public, including men having sex with men, though in some big cities special services exist exclusively for them. It is impossible, in this report, to take account of the experiences of all these different services. Many of them keep records of the number, the main characteristics of the callers, and sometimes their demands. Although local specificities are very important, the evolution of the demands also reveals important similarities between countries, including North America and Australia. During the first years of AIDS work, the rate of increase in calls from year to year is often exponential. An example is the Paris AIDES hot line. The number of callers rose from 1,000 calls in 1985 to 3,840 in 1986, and 8,641 in 1987, and has stabilized on this level since then. At times of intensive media reporting (e.g., at the occasion of the International Conference on AIDS), hot line activities peak. In the first years, most calls came from concerned homo- and bisexual men (sex ratio: 25 percent female, 75 percent male). The dominant age group is 25 to 45 years, most people call for themselves, and most calls last less than 15 minutes, though some run up to 45 minutes. When, in 1987, the government started its TV campaigns, the sex ratio slowly changed as more women used the service. Also, the proportion of seropositive callers slowly decreased. From the search for medical information and for certainty about means of HIV transmission, the inquiries became more diffuse, sometimes taking the form of a confession. Good psychological skills and training of the volunteer respondents are essential. Sometimes callers are referred to medical or psychological specialists. At the end of 1990, with the help of AIDES, the French Agency for Prevention (AFLS) launched a free nationwide AIDS hot line responsible for educating the respondents. In Berlin, a 24-hour hot line was used by 71 percent men and 29 percent women, 73 percent defining themselves as heterosexuals and 27 percent as gay. Most calls concerned the means of transmission and the test. Heterosexuals often expressed unspecific fears and problems in partner relationships, while many homosexuals had more practical problems about how to deal with seropositivity, where to find treatments, etc. (Pollak and Rosman, 1989).

Specific hot lines for men having sex with men, in Paris, Amsterdam, and Berlin, have registered a growing number of inquiries about sexual dysfunctions and psychological distress directly attributable to the epidemic, to the number of deaths in the gay environment, and, eventually, to one's own seropositivity.

Outreach Work

We can distinguish two broad categories in outreach work:

- actions through which one tries to mobilize support for HIV prevention programs from outside the most concerned segment of the population,
- actions through which one tries to educate people who are hard to reach by traditional information and communication approaches.

Mobilization of financial support from outside the most exposed groups has contributed to consciousness raising, social tolerance and solidarity. These actions have been of paramount importance in countries where public authorities contribute little to developing the sector of voluntary associations. Such actions usually link information and education with fund raising. In the United Kingdom, street festivals, rock concerts, and public auctions have been organized for such purposes with great success. Well-known stars such as Vanessa Redgrave and Boy George have actively participated and become disseminators of the prevention message. In Paris, AIDES has motivated restaurants to participate in the World AIDS day, December first. These actions began in Parisian gay establishments, and others joined in the second year. The patrons of the restaurants pay a part of the day's earnings to AIDS organizations. In addition, clients are asked to give some additional support. The financial resources collected this way are not the only benefits of such actions, for people participating engage in discussions and speak very freely about changes in attitudes and sexual behavior. This can reinforce their personal willingness and capacity for safer sex compliance.

In Austria, a few actors have conceived sketches for street theater. They perform during rush hours in the center of Vienna and in subway stations. In a few countries, TV shows also combine information, education, and fund raising.

Outreach programs inside the gay community for people who are hard to reach extend efforts to access men having sex with men that started in gay newspapers, bars, and discos. Each time activists wanted to distribute prevention materials and enter into discussions with isolated gay men, they had to overcome barriers. In the early years of the epidemic, some gay magazines, bars, and discos were reluctant to help because they anticipated AIDS information in their establishments would have negative effects on their income. As the epidemic became more visible, in the mid-1980s, gay establishments joined the cause. The major problem today is reaching men having sex with men who do not read the gay press and who do not go to gay establishments. Their proportion is very difficult to evaluate. If one combines different sources of information (snowball sampling surveys, newspaper surveys, qualitative interviewing), one finds that a vast majority of men having sex with men have no continuous relationship with community establishments; among respondents to a French newspaper survey (Pollak and Schiltz, 1991), more than half of respondents are only occasional readers. According to the same survey, only 30 percent go to a gay bar, disco or sauna at least once a month. Only seven percent participate in gay organizations, six percent in AIDS organizations. In a quota sampling control survey among 300 gay men, relationships with gay community life are significantly lower. Based on these indications, one could estimate that 60 to 80 percent of men having sex with men have no or only occasional links with a structured, organized gay community.

Street worker programs, developed for IVDUs, became a reference model for work in public places and in toilets where men meet for occasional, anonymous sex. The AIDS Council of New South Wales in Australia has conceived and evaluated its innovative approach which became a reference document for many gay AIDS organizations (van Reyk et al., 1990). This program started in 1988. AIDS educators systematically distribute safer sex educational materials (stickers, badges, leaflets) and try to establish communication with men coming for sex to public places, toilets in subway stations, department stores, and parks. This approach implies an insider knowledge of the functioning of such places: some are busy in the morning hours, some at lunch hours, and some in the evening or late at night. The clients coming at different hours are not necessarily the same.

Establishing contacts and getting into a conversation is often very difficult, as most people come for anonymous, rapid sex. As the interview work showed, many of them hide their homosexuality, many are married. For some, the interview was the first occasion in their life for speaking about their sexual life to a sympathetic ear. This face to face interaction included:

- discussion of HIV transmission,
- discussion of individual's perception of his own risk,
- clarification of safer sex practices,
- discussion of safe needle use (for homosexual IVDUs).

Another objective of the project was to break the self-isolation of many of these men in order to develop peer support for safer sex practices among the target group. This last point was the most difficult, if not impossible, to achieve, as it implies disclosure of one's own homosexuality. There is no possibility for a reliable statistical validation of these observations, but according to the authors, "Evidence suggests that the project has contributed to an increase in the field of knowledge of safe sexual practices and a decrease in the frequency of unsafe sexual activities among users." Nevertheless, the Sydney study also points to the persistence of high levels of unsafe practices and the difficulty of changing to safer sex in the absence of peer support. Their study also revealed the difficulty of contacting working class men as well as men from non-English speaking backgrounds. Similar experimental programs are presently underway in Austria, Denmark, France, Germany, Switzerland, the Netherlands, Norway, Quebec, and now in the United Kingdom as well.

Another problem addressed by the Sydney study is the relationship with the police: "Approaching police is seen as a two-edged sword. Police have had an unfortunate history of harassment, raids and entrapment associated with beats (toilets) and these are very much current issues for the project. Informing police may serve to draw attention to a beat rather than anything else. Legislation against (homo)sexual acts, soliciting or public nuisance where it exists of course places police in a difficult position in supporting a project for beat users" (van Reyk et al., 1990). This sentence not only applies to public toilets, but to all forms of meeting places offering occasions for sexual contacts. The rules differ among European countries.

Sexual Meeting Places

The liberalization of the last twenty years in most West European countries has favored the emergence of a diversified infrastructure of bars, restaurants, and discos specializing in a gay clientele. Meeting places in general play a privileged role in a global approach to prevention. Bars, discos, and restaurants have participated in prevention by distributing leaflets, displaying safer sex posters, and organizing conferences and discussions or fund raising dinners for AIDS organizations. These activities have become major moments of community solidarity. They also help to access the diverse male homo- and bisexual population.

Some of these establishments offer on-the-spot facilities for sexual encounters. In particular, backrooms and bathhouses have been accused of being centers of sexual transmission of the HIV. Such establishments are not specific to gay life; they also exist for a heterosexual clientele, but in the debate on HIV prevention, most criticisms concentrate exclusively on gay establishments. In the United States, controversies have resulted in the closing of many bathhouses (Perrow and Guillen, 1990).

Should one control them, how can compliance to safer sex rules in such places be guaranteed? These were the questions put forward in the debate. In most countries, such facilities for sexual activities are tolerated by police and not definitively accepted by law (Coxon, Davies, and McManus, 1990). Rare and illegal in the United Kingdom, they are common in Germany, the Netherlands, Denmark, Switzerland, France, Italy, and Spain, where such places mushroomed in the post-Franco years. Most gay activists and many prevention specialists are opposed to repressive arguments.

As far as backrooms and bathhouses are concerned, different approaches prevailed in different countries. As early as 1985 the health authorities and the police in the Netherlands and one of the Swiss cantons signed agreements with the patrons of such places or their representatives. According to these agreements, the patrons offered their active participation in prevention (information and condom promotion); public authorities, in turn, agreed to restrain from coercive action. This approach is favored, in the case of the Netherlands, by the existence of a representative organization of gay patrons able to negotiate and speak in the name of the profession. Most Dutch and Swiss saunas have participated in prevention actions, in particular condom promotion.

A press campaign initiated in Sweden by a well-known journalist resulted in the closing of a Stockholm bathhouse. Gay activists insisted on the counterproductive nature of such repressive action with its negative effects on the climate of confidence between gay organizations and public authorities.

In Finland, the gay organization SETA runs the major places for gay socializing (bars and discos). SETA tried to negotiate compliance with safer sex rules in a private gay sauna in Helsinki. When the patrons refused, SETA itself contributed to its voluntary closing a few months later. In Bavaria, the police abstained from officially closing bathhouses, but frequent controls led to closings by the patrons themselves.

In most countries the situation remains ambiguous. In France, a telephone survey conducted during a targeted information campaign for men having sex with men showed interesting results in early 1990. All known gay establishments were asked to display the safer sex poster used for this campaign. More than 80 percent of establishments did so. But when asked if they would participate in condom promotion and regularly sell condoms in their establishment, the proportion of potential participants is significantly lower in establishments where sexual activities do take place. The reasons for this paradoxical situation are commercial ("our clients come to relax") and legal. Many patrons fear that the sale of condoms could be interpreted as an act of procurement and used against them by the police. Clearly, the undefined legal status between tolerance and acceptance can have negative effects on prevention. A seminar bringing together AIDS activists, patrons, and representatives of the police allowed these people to discuss this problem and, at least, to make it explicit. A few positive results came out of these discussions: gay patrons created a professional association allowing them to negotiate collectively with public authorities; this in turn, reassured them that AIDS prevention in their establishment could not be interpreted as procurement and used against them.

GENERAL VERSUS TARGETED APPROACHES

On a formal level, AIDS prevention approaches do not differ substantially among European countries. Almost everywhere we find leaflets, posters, videos, condom handouts, hot lines, newsletters, etc. Over the last years, outreach programs and safer sex workshops were added to more traditional information approaches. For the moment limited to a few countries, they probably will soon spread to southern Europe. National approaches differ in explicitness and in the definition of the meaning of "targeting," strongly correlated with the organizational preconditions for prevention discussed in the first part of this report.

In a few countries where there is a high degree of social integration and tolerant attitudes toward homosexuality and homosexual men prevail, we observe close cooperation between public authorities and gay community representatives with regard to the dissemination of messages. Targeting then becomes a technical question of how to provide these messages to as many people as possible. Examples are the Netherlands and Denmark. Diverse opinions between authorities and gay organizations about messages were small and so were tolerated and expressed. Knowledge, Attitude, Belief, Practice (KABP) surveys among gay men attest to a high degree of confidence in public authorities and in voluntary associations. This consensual approach is favored by a long tradition of sex education. National television, general media, and gay media were perceived as equally useful sources in a Danish survey, the general national campaign even had slightly better scores in reaching all segments of the gay population under survey. On the other hand, much more satisfaction was expressed by those using the gay safer sex information (Bottzauw, Hermansen, and Tauris, 1989a and b). In the Netherlands, generally distributed materials can mention and explicitly show same-sex practices without provoking countermobilization or lobbying.

In other countries with less consensual coordination and traditions between health authorities and the voluntary sector, "targeting" also refers to the style and the content of messages. In Germany, the Deutsche AIDS-Hilfe has defined itself more and more as the representative of the interests of the most exposed groups and the infected. Here "targeting" refers not only to accessing the concerned populations, but to the conception of specific messages and images. While Deutsche AIDS-Hilfe materials are explicit, including pornographic condom videoclips, health administrations use more neutral leaflets and advertisements.

In France, AIDES pursues a general approach which does not differentiate groups in terms of messages, attempting instead to improve access to people who are difficult to reach, as surveys revealed a slower adaptation to the risk of transmission in France than in its neighboring countries. The public authorities have accepted, in 1989, the principle of specific, very explicit, safer sex materials for men having sex with men, produced together with several gay organizations responsible for distribution. Studies have examined the effects on gay people of prevention campaigns directed toward the general population. In France and Germany, KABP surveys in the male homo- and bisexual population reveal that the general press and the gay media have comparable high levels as sources of information (from 70 to 80 percent). In Germany, the Deutsche AIDS-Hilfe, with its targeted materials, is a source for more than 50 percent of respondents while voluntary associations such as AIDES, that largely refused group-specific discourses, represent only 11 percent in France. Nevertheless, even in France the gay press (65 percent) and voluntary associations (54 percent) enjoy higher credibility among gay men than the general press (22 percent) or the public authorities (Bochow, 1989; Pollak, 1989).

In France, surveys were conducted at the same time and using the same questions in a representative sample of the adult population over 18 and among the respondents of a gay newspaper (Pollak, 1989; Moatti et al., 1990). These surveys show that male homo- and bisexuals have perceived more than the general population the two TV campaigns, one on condoms, the other on solidarity with seropositives (93 versus 71 percent). Only 49 percent of the general population, but 75 percent among male homo- and bisexuals, felt themselves personally concerned by these campaigns. Nevertheless, gays formulate more skeptical judgements than the general population on the effectiveness of these TV campaigns in 1988 and 1989. Of respondents in the general population, 66 percent, as compared to only 35 percent in the gay group, thought that these campaigns have had a positive effect on the level of knowledge. These campaigns had only limited effects on sexual behavior changes–according to both surveys 12 percent started using condoms. While this reflects a lack of feeling of personal exposure in the general population, in the gay population it reveals a high level of behavioral change achieved much earlier. Even in the gay population, the campaigns had a very positive effect on the maintenance of a high level of awareness and on the regularity of safer sex. In 1988, 18 percent, and, in 1989, 38 percent of the respondents of the yearly survey of readers of the French gay press (Pollak and Schiltz, 1991) answered that the public campaigns have reinforced their positive attitudes toward safer sex and helped them to practice it more regularly. This comparison between Germany and France teaches us a few lessons. In both countries, the gay community is fragmented into very small organizations, social attitudes toward homosexuality are comparable, and voluntary associations, faced with the inactivity of public authorities, became major actors in the field of prevention. Each country, however, adopted very different strategies. With high official financial support, the German AIDS-Hilfe used group-specific languages and messages, while the lack of specificity of the materials produced by the French organization AIDES has limited its efficiency for the most exposed groups. It was under the auspices of public authorities advised by a group of gay experts that more specific arguments and materials could be introduced in 1989 (Pollak, Pelé et al., 1990).

The picture is quite different in Ireland. While 80 percent of respondents to a survey organized by "Gay Health Action" judged very useful the information work achieved by gay organizations, only 38 percent did so for the government campaign which had used moralizing arguments (GHA Survey Results, 1989).

In all countries, the effectiveness of AIDS prevention was improved by different forms of community mobilization. According to surveys in the gay population, the preventive role of general physicians, in contrast, is limited in all countries. Less than 20 percent in Denmark, 25 percent in France, 14 percent in Germany, 29 percent in Ireland, and 29 percent in Switzerland indicate them as useful sources for information.

These empirical data allow us to more precisely formulate the meaning of targeting and the conditions for effective prevention:

- The structured organization of minorities is a prerequisite for their social and political integration into the larger society. For organizing itself, a minority tends to stress its specificities and identity. The better its social organization and its bargaining power in society, the less important the need for the minority to insist on its specificities. Where homosexual themes can be freely addressed in general materials, such as in the Netherlands and Denmark, "targeting" is basically a technical question of multiplying the channels of distribution.
- Where gay organizational infrastructure and bargaining power is weak and social integration still fragile, AIDS organizations play an important role in community empowerment, as in Germany, Ireland, and the United Kingdom. "Targeting" is then a question not only of the distribution, but of the conception of different content in prevention materials, explicitly stressing gay themes. Here autonomous strategies insisting on group identities and using specific arguments have been particularly efficient. Such an active and aggressive attitude prevails where homosexuality, for political and legal reasons, is culturally defined as a political and collective issue. In an adversarial climate, this emancipatory group-specific approach is reinforced in Ireland and the United Kingdom by the arguments used in government campaigns (fear, monogamy, sexual abstinence), and in Germany by the example of Bavaria with its coercive approach toward prevention.
- In France, group-specific, identity-based arguments are generally perceived as illegitimate. The weakness of social organizations able to mediate between the State and the citizen reflects this tradition. In addition, sexuality is culturally defined exclusively in terms of personal choice. This explains two specific features of the French history of AIDS work: the inability of government to conceive targeted strategies and its tendency to rely on a biomedical approach, and the unwillingness of the major voluntary association AIDES to conceive group-specific rhetorics and strategies (Pollak, 1988b). Only very recently have

both government and the voluntary sector changed this approach under the pressure of the rapid development of the epidemic.

- Similar situations prevail in Mediterranean Europe. In Italy, Spain, and Portugal the lobbying power of the Catholic Church adds to sociocultural factors that limit targeted approaches of men having sex with men. The refusal of many men having sex with men to identify themselves as gay or homosexual is reinforced by the absence of a structured gay community. As in France, health officials in charge of AIDS have understood their own interest for organized partners as multipliers of the health message. Often they have become advocates of a liberal, sexually explicit prevention approach implemented at the local or regional levels. Even where practical realizations have remained minimal, such as in Greece and Portugal, public officials often underline in interviews the "excellent work achieved by the gay communities in their country." If one adopts a critical attitude, one might interpret this sentence as cheap lip service. Our impression is rather more optimistic: the experience of individual discussions with openly gay men has lifted social barriers and opened a willingness for positive cooperation, difficult to implement in the absence of community representatives.

- With the differentiation and multiplication of diverse channels of information, the risk of contradictory messages increases. We have observed contradictory prevention philosophies in a few countries as well as contradictory messages about transmission. This undermines credibility and confidence and should be avoided.

- "Targeting" is usually defined in terms of accessing a specific group in the field of information dissemination. The group "men having sex with men" is not homogeneous. It includes self-identifying, urban gays with a middle-class background, specific "scenes" (leather, S-M groups, etc.) with ritualized forms of sexual practices, and also married men and isolated men occasionally having sex with other men in public places. Targeting also must take into account these distinctions inside the male homo- and bisexual population, primarily in terms of multiplying the channels for distributing the prevention message: general and gay media, the handing out of leaflets and condoms in all types of meeting places, voluntary associations, etc.

- Given the high levels of basic information on the ways of transmission, general mass media (TV and newspapers) today fulfill an important function for maintaining a high level of risk awareness. For behavior changes and their reinforcement, community-based communication networks are more helpful.
- For the above-mentioned reason, TV campaigns should be organized on a regular continuous level, and not concentrated around single events.
- Group-specific approaches become essential if one no longer exclusively defines prevention as information dissemination, but in terms of interactive and/or ritualized learning of new behaviors. This is the case of most safer sex workshops, of Jack-off clubs, but also of self-support groups whose members often insist on a specific composition according to gender, sexual preference or, in the case of seropositives, transmission modalities.

TESTING POLICIES

When the HIV-antibody test first became available on a large scale (in most countries in between 1984 and early 1985), hospitals, prisons, and institutions dealing with IVDUs often administered the test without prior informed consent. Testing as part of employment or civil service tenure decisions have been discovered in the cities of Paris and Vienna. AIDS organizations denounced such practices, and defined and helped implement ethical rules: informed consent, voluntariness, and respect for medical confidentiality.

In addition, most AIDS organizations were reluctant or openly hostile toward mass testing programs in the absence of treatment possibilities. In the Netherlands, this anti-test position was formally endorsed by the national AIDS council.

In a few countries, this position is now being softened and changed. Early recognition, not only of clinical symptoms, but of biological markers, permits early intervention and retroviral treatments that help to avoid or at least delay opportunistic diseases.

Psychological stress was another reason for a cautious approach toward the test. The discovery of a positive test result might induce depression, self-isolation and, indirectly, negatively affect the immune system. How could it be guaranteed that the results would remain secret without adverse effects on the social position of the HIV positive patient? Therefore, the creation of anonymous test sites providing individual pre- and post-test counseling became a major issue. These now exist in most countries. They are run on an informal basis by gay health services, by medical associations such as Medecins du Monde in France or formally managed by the health authorities. In Finland, where the social security number of all persons testing positive is registered, an exception has been granted to the Finnish AIDS Information and Support Center which has temporary permission to carry out completely anonymous testing in five cities. This center has been established at the initiative of SETA. The Austria AIDS-Hilfe is responsible for anonymous testing offered in the capital cities of the country's nine Länder.

Counseling efforts are still insufficient. According to a German survey (Bochow, 1990b), over half of the tests were not accompanied by counseling. In Ireland the figure is 53 percent. Of the Irish gays who did benefit from counseling, only 62 percent were satisfied with what counseling they received (GHA, 1989).

Compulsory testing programs either presently exist or are systematically proposed for specific groups: registered prostitutes (Austria, Athens-Greece, Bavaria), IVDUs (Bavaria, Ireland, Italy), and civil servants (Bavaria). Foreign students with scholarships must be tested or made to prove their seronegativity in Germany, Belgium, United Kingdom, and Greece.

According to Swedish law every person suspected of carrying a disease that is "dangerous to the society" must be examined by a physician. If the test is negative, anonymity is guaranteed. In the case of a positive result, the person is registered and the physician is obliged to trace contact and to submit the sexual partners to the HIV antibody test, if necessary with the help of the police. As in Bavaria, the physician must give the patient behavioral prescriptions. Noncompliance with these rules can lead to loss of confidentiality and a quarantine of the patient. Under the pressure of some segments of the medical profession, similar provisions are being discussed in Finland. As a result of such repressive policies, or of fear of disclosure, people go to other countries for voluntary testing, into the neighboring Länder in the case of Bavaria, to Norway or Denmark in the case of Sweden. The size of these movements is difficult to evaluate. Ten percent of respondents to the GHA Survey in Ireland took the test outside the country. Such repressive actions have deeply affected the confidence of voluntary associations in public authorities.

In some countries, e.g., Finland, it is quite commonplace to offer "routine" testing in situations where it is difficult to refuse, such as in maternity clinics for expectant mothers, army recruits, health inspections in some large companies, and secret HIV testing of black Africans (although this was apparently discontinued after a demonstration against the racism inherent in this practice). In all these circumstances, especially the army, it is practically impossible to refuse the test. Additional problems are caused by the fact that the personnel performing routine tests are not trained for the complicated situation of administering HIV tests and giving results. Usually no pre- or post-test counseling is associated with these routine tests and no psychological support is available. Results are still sometimes given by phone.

In some instances, the test results are made public in a way which endangers personal confidentiality. As an example, the Finnish UN soldiers who returned from their duty abroad were subjected to routine testing in the summer of 1990. The exact number of HIV positives, the name of the military unit, and the name of the country where they had served was published in the press. In France, soldiers on duty in Africa are also routinely tested.

According to national KABP surveys, a very high proportion of male homo- and bisexuals have already been tested (Table 4). Only in countries where AIDS organizations and public authorities hold a common skeptical position toward testing is the proportion of tested gay men significantly lower (Netherlands) (Tielman and Polter, 1988). In Germany (Bochow, 1988) and France (Pollak and Schiltz, 1991), more than 50 percent of respondents had taken the test at least once as of 1988, and by 1990 this proportion rose to 72 percent

TABLE 4. Self-reported test results.

	UK (1988)[1]	Netherlands (1987)[2]	Ireland (1988)[3]	Germany (1988)[4]	Switzerland (1990)[5]	France (1990)[6]	Italy (1989)[7]
Nontested	58%	83%	60%	43%	33%	28%	52%
Tested	42%	17%	40%	57%	67%	72%	48%
HIV+ of tested men	9%	12%	9%	13%	13%	19%	4%
	(n = 1339)	(n = 522)	(n = 265)	(n = 1122)	(n = 720)	(n = 2000)	(n = 1340)

1. McManus, McEvans
2. R. Tielman, S. Polter
3. Gay Health Action
4. M. Bochow
5. J. B. Masur; 6% did not give the test result
6. M. Pollak
7. H. Sasse, et al.; 9% did not give the test result

in France. The Oslo municipality's AIDS center approached all gay bars and discos each weekend in the spring of 1990. To find the frequency of testing, 1,082 forms were distributed. Of the 741 respondents, 76 percent had already been tested. In the Mediterranean South figures are lower. In Italy, for example, only 48 percent of gay men had been tested as of 1989 (Sasse et al., 1990).

Empirical evidence suggests that the decision to take the test is heavily influenced by perceived risk behavior, such as unprotected anal intercourse and number of partners. In France, where 30 percent of survey respondents had already taken the test by 1986, this tendency is well documented. Voluntary testing started among gays with the highest level of sexual activity, including risky practices, in big urban centers and in the highly educated middle classes (Pollak and Schiltz, 1988). As the tested population became larger, including less exposed segments of the gay population, self-reported seroprevalence rates decreased from 23 percent in 1986 to 19 percent in 1990. Self-reported seroprevalence rates were lower in Germany (13 percent) among tested male homo- and bisexuals. In the Netherlands (Tielman and Polter, 1988), a similar proportion was measured on a much smaller basis of tested people (17 percent as against 60 percent in Germany [Bochow, 1988] and France [Pollak and Schiltz, 1991]). In England and Ireland (GHA, 1989), one finds even lower seroprevalence rates of some ten percent, in Italy of four percent (Sasse et al., 1990). These country differences in self-reported serostatus are coherent with AIDS-surveillance statistics. Although survey methods with self-reported test results do not allow us to precisely measure HIV incidence, they allow us to follow HIV diffusion trends. Therefore, they are an efficient early warning system.

All seroprevalence data have recruitment biases. In general, the more "specific" the recruitment of the population under observation, the higher the seroprevalence rate. Particularly high in VD clinics and epidemiological cohort studies recruiting participants among people seeking care, these rates are lower in self-reported sociological surveys. Sampling differences account for these variations much more than systematic response biases linked to hiding.

Another phenomenon well-documented in French surveys is the massive entry of gay men into medical surveillance. Half of the tested respondents have undergone the test more than once. Several phenomena account for this: almost all seropositives, asymptomatic or not, enter medical surveillance based on regular serological and immunological tests; some people also take the test to reassure themselves from time to time. In a minority group with unsafe sex behavior, repeated testing is used as an instrument for managing fears of infection. This attitude clearly demonstrates that testing does not automatically reinforce protective behaviors (Siegel et al., 1989).

To determine whether voluntary testing assists prevention, studies compared the sexual behavior of untested and tested seronegative and seropositive male homo- and bisexuals. These studies indicated more behavior changes among people who tested positive than those who tested negative. Tested people also showed more changes than untested ones. Nevertheless, these differences are very difficult to interpret as van Griensven writes in a Dutch study: "Apart from serological testing and its results, many other factors might have influenced the behaviour of the men under study. Counseling for example may interact with the effect of testing itself . . . Because the ethical and practical considerations prohibit experimenting with the factors mentioned above, their individual contribution to the effect of testing cannot be distinguished" (van Griensven et al., 1989).

A French study comes to similar conclusions: "There is no clear causal relationship between testing and safer sex. Rather the same sociocultural factors are conducive to taking the test and to starting safer sex:

- a realistic assessment of one's risk exposure;
- high education and middle class background;
- social acceptance of one's homosexuality and the capacity for safer sex negotiation (Pollak and Schiltz, 1988)."

All available empirical evidence suggests that complete compliance to safer sex is extremely difficult to achieve and to maintain. Even in the seropositive group, eight percent of respondents in the French survey of 1990 maintain at least some unsafe behavior (unprotected anal intercourse). We find the same proportion among HIV-respondents. This proportion rises to 13 percent in the non-tested group.

This situation has evolved considerably over the years. The more safer sex becomes a social norm, generally accepted and reinforced in the gay community, the less these three groups, untested, tested HIV+, and tested HIV-, differ from each other. (See Table 5.)

TABLE 5. Risk taking and HIV status.

	1987	1990
Not tested	55%	13%
HIV negative	51%	8%
HIV positive	36%	8%

Source: Pollak, Schiltz, 1991. We define "risk takers" as people with sexual relationships outside a closed couple relationship with known serostatus practicing always or sometimes unprotected anal intercourse.

Therefore, testing cannot be considered as a prevention instrument in itself. Only in relation with counseling can it become a privileged moment for reinforcing safer behavior.

We can conclude:

- Depending on the social climate surrounding it, voluntary testing is widespread among men having sex with men. We observe a quest for certainty in a situation of psychological stress. This quest is presently reinforced by the logic of early therapeutic intervention in case of seropositivity.
- Where not yet existing, alternative anonymous test sites should be created.
- Compulsory testing can have adverse effects; it should be banned on ethical grounds.
- Routine testing in situations where it is difficult to refuse can have the same adverse effects as compulsory testing, especially since the personnel administering routine tests do not have the required training.
- There have been reports of the publication of the test results of certain subgroups with such detail that it may endanger ano-

nymity. It is strongly suggested that HIV-figures be published on aggregate levels only.

- Clear ethical rules should be followed in all testing programs: informed consent, confidentiality, medical secrecy.
- Testing should be accompanied by pre- and post-test counseling.
- Some evidence suggests a positive effect of the voluntary test on sexual behavior change, but further evidence is needed for interpreting these data.

Part Two:
Assessing Knowledge, Attitudes, and Behavior Changes

RESEARCH STRATEGIES

The AIDS epidemic has provoked a proliferation of research projects not only in the biomedical field and in epidemiology, but also in social sciences. As the most infected group, male homo- and bisexuals have become major subjects for investigation. In most European countries, such research has been undertaken by independent researchers, by AIDS organizations, and by gay associations and media or in close cooperation with them. Long-term funding for non-medical research has often been difficult to obtain and secure. Evaluation of specific prevention instruments and campaigns is exceptional.

If changes in HIV-incidence is the major goal of prevention, national surveillance systems are not sensitive enough to measure them precisely and even less able to measure the effects of general and/or group-specific interventions. In addition to prevention programs, an environment of intense media coverage influences people's attitudes and behaviors. Diverse prevention programs start at the same periods without the possibility of proper evaluation of each particular project. In retrospect, the observed knowledge and behavior can only be interpreted as the result of numerous formal and informal interventions and experiences, of a prevention climate basically informed by country-specific policies and media reporting.

The design of major research projects reflects the state of the epidemic. Before 1985 epidemiological cohort studies were initiated with the objective of identifying different risk factors and practices, and monitoring sexual behavior changes and their impact on HIV incidence rates among homo- and bisexual men. Later sociological surveys became interested in the determinants and parameters of sexual behavior changes. Besides sexual practices and their modifications, these surveys investigate sociocultural variables: the level of AIDS knowledge, the sources of information used, social networks, acceptance of homosexuality, and self-esteem. In the WHO terminology, these surveys are called KABP (Knowledge, Attitudes, Beliefs, Practices). For more precise measurement, a British research team used the sexual diary approach.

Sociologists, anthropologists, and social psychologists have approached the same questions with qualitative research methodologies. These more qualitatively-based studies using indepth interviews and participant observation can clarify the meaning of the changes that affect gay life. An understanding of personality and social network variables related to behavior change can help shed light on the resistance to change and the emotional stress and loss involved in changing behavior and in experiencing death in one's close environment.

The countries where the gay population is the most severely hit by the epidemic have developed the most complete set of research projects, allowing them to monitor changes and to orient their prevention policies: the Netherlands, Denmark, France, Switzerland, Germany, and the United Kingdom. In most other countries KABP surveys are either under way or in preparation. In many countries, this will be the first time that homosexual behavior and living conditions are empirically researched.

SAMPLING

All research on male homo- and bisexuals (Table 6) has to overcome similar problems of sampling and biases inherent in self-reported data on practices that are not accepted socially and sometimes suffer discrimination. For longitudinal purposes, cohort members are usually recruited through health services, VD clinics, or networks of gay doctors. In Amsterdam, the recruitment of 741 male homosexuals in 1984 was possible because of the relationship between the Municipal Health Service and the male homosexual community during several epidemiologic and prevention studies of STDs (van Griensven et al., 1987). In Denmark, a cohort of 260 gay men, members of LBL, was composed in 1982 and observed since then (Melbye, 1989; Ebbensen, 1988). In both cases, cohort participants were unmarried, professional, and highly educated. In addition to blood samples for determining HIV-antibody status, these studies investigate sociodemographic, psychological, life style, and sexual behavior in order to isolate risk practices and to determine the correlations between HIV status and behavior.

Quantitative investigations such as KABP surveys among gay men always pose the problem that since the ambit of the group cannot be known, representative sampling cannot be undertaken. As representativeness is impossible to achieve, one can try to get a sample large enough to guarantee significant statistical results and to reflect the diversity of the population under study. The problem then becomes access. In countries with a dense organizational network with high membership rates, large samples can be constituted by distributing questionnaires. Inserting a questionnaire in gay magazines is another way to access the gay population. These two approaches privilege people with a certain gay self-consciousness expressed in membership or readership of specialized organizations and media. Another way of accessing gays is to put in different meeting places questionnaires that they are asked to send back to the research team.

In snowball sampling, the research team constitutes a network of collaborators at different localities who hand out a certain number of questionnaires to other men having sex with men and ask them to do the same with other men they know. Quota sampling of male homo- and bisexuals proceeds the same way as quota sampling in the general population. Quotas are modeled according to the sociodemographic characteristics of the male population: age, profession, educational level, and residence. Interviewers are then asked to find men having sex with men who fit these different quotas. All of these sampling techniques have been used. The choices reflect pragmatic constraints and/or hypotheses about the segments of the population reached by these different approaches. The experiences of the last years allow us to better analyze the biases of different sampling procedures.

In countries where gay magazines have a limited circulation and associations are very small, distributing questionnaires in meeting

TABLE 6. Major studies available in Europe.

Country	Year	Type of study	N	Sample Methodology	Authors
Austria	1990	KABP (in progress)	270	Snowball	Dür et al.
Belgium	1986	KABP	200	Snowball	Univ. of Louvain
	1990	KABP	379	Snowball	Vincke
Denmark	1982	Cohort	260	Cohort	Melbye et al.
	1988	KABP	2100	Gay Organ	Schmidt et al.
Finland	1990	KABP (in progress)	160	Snowball	Grönfors
France	1985	KABP + int	1000	Newspaper	Pollak et al.
	1986	KABP	1200	Newspaper	Pollak et al.
	1987	KABP	1200	Newspaper	Pollak et al.
	1988	KABP	1500	Newspaper	Pollak et al.
	1989	KABP + int	1500	Newspaper	Pollak et al.
	1990	KABP + int	2200	Newspaper	Pollak et al.
Germany	1987	KABP	924	Newspaper	Bochow
	1988	KABP	1122	Newspaper	Bochow
	1988	KABP	903	Snowball	Dannecker
Ireland	1988	KABP	265	Snowball	Gay Health Action

Italy	1989	KABP	Snowball	1340	Sasse et al.
Netherlands	1984	Cohort	Cohort	741	Van Griesven et al.
	1986	KABP	Newspaper	522	Tielman et al.
	1987	KABP	Newspaper	522	Tielman et al.
	1990	KABP	Newspaper	522	Tielman et al.
Norway	1986	Interviews	Bars, Disco	60	Prieur
Portugal	1990	Interviews (in progress)	Bars, Disco	?	
Sweden	1990	Interviews (in progress)		?	
Switzerland	1987	KABP + int	Newspaper	795	Dubois et al.
	1990	KABP + int	Newspaper	720	Masur et al.
United Kingdom	1985	KABP	Newspaper	1267	McManus et al.
	1988	KABP	Newspaper	1339	McManus et al.
	1988	Sexual diary	Snowball	170	Coxon et al.

No major assessment/research projects specifically concerned with gay men were reported from Greece, Luxembourg, and Spain. This table is not exhaustive: in particular local projects were not taken into consideration, only projects completed or in a final stage at the end of 1990 are listed.

places is the preferred means for recruiting large numbers of respondents. In Ireland, a sample size of 265 respondents has been reached in 1988, the first research sample of this kind in the country (GHA Survey Results, 1989). A large portion of respondents (44 percent) were approached in Dublin bars. Therefore, the sample is representative of Dublin (79% of the respondents) than of the whole country, for the age group 20-29 (50 percent) and 30-39 (34 percent). Similar sample biases for residence and age were observed in a French survey of 1983 that used the same sampling approach (Cavailhès, Dutey, and Bach-Ignasse, 1984). Local studies have been organized in Belgium. The largest study in the gay population was organized in the Flemish-speaking part of the country. A snowball system recruited 379 people who were interviewed on motivations for adopting or not adopting safer sex (Vincke, Mak, and Bolton, 1991).

Because of their wide circulation, newspaper samples succeed in reaching much larger numbers of respondents and segments of the population. In Denmark, 2,100 male homo- and bisexuals answered a questionnaire enclosed in two national gay magazines in the spring of 1988. Among the respondents were 66 percent of male members of the national gay and lesbian organization LBL, regional and age distribution was satisfactory (Schmidt, unpublished data). In Italy, the first large survey on gay life in 1987 resulted from a three-partner cooperation, the largest gay association Arci Gay, a research institute ISPES, and the magazine *Epoca*. Ten thousand questionnaires were distributed through diverse channels; 1,743 were returned and analyzed. A third of the respondents were Arci Gay members (Carreta, Manzoni, 1990). A second survey was organized by Arci Gay and the Istituto Superiore di Sanita in 1989. Three-thousand questionnaires were distributed through diverse channels in all regions; 1,340 were returned and analyzed (Sasse et al., 1990).

In the United Kingdom, McManus and McEvoy (1987) enclosed a questionnaire in a gay magazine and received 1,267 responses in 1985 and 1,339 in 1988. In Germany, Michael Bochow organized two newspaper surveys for the German AIDS-Hilfe, the first in 1987, the second in 1988 when he also circulated the questionnaire in leather bars and saunas to better represent this specific segment of the population. He used seven gay magazines and reached 924 respondents in 1987 and 1,122 in 1988 (Bochow, 1988; Bochow, 1989). In France, Michael Pollak from the National Scientific Research Center (CNRS) organized a yearly survey among the readers of the gay magazine *Gai Pied Hebdo*. From 1,000 respondents in 1985, this number increased to more than 2,000 in 1987, the year of the first national campaigns, and then stabilized above 1,500 per year. Each year the first 1,200, 1,500 or 2,000 responses were used for statistical analysis (Pollak, 1988b; Pollak, Schiltz, and Laurinda, 1986; Pollak and Schiltz, 1991).

In the Netherlands, the gay studies program at the University of Utrecht enclosed a questionnaire in the gay national magazine *De Gay Krant* and asked organizations to send it out to their members. This procedure was repeated in 1986, 1987, and 1988. Only the respondents of all these waves were used for statistical panel analysis (Tielman and Polter, 1988). In Switzerland, Françoise Dubois-Arber, D. Franck and Jean-Blaise Masur of the Institute of Social and Preventive Medicine used a similar approach in 1987 and 1990, enclosing the questionnaire in four gay magazines and distributing it through gay organizations. They received 795 responses in 1987 and 720 in 1990 (Dubois-Arber and Franck, 1987).

These newspaper surveys over-represent middle class gays with high levels of education. They hardly reach blue collar and immigrant labor. The age distribution from 18 to 50 years is generally satisfactory. Depending on the circulation, newspaper samples sometimes over-represent the major cities and urban regions. Where there have been repeated surveys (France, Netherlands, Germany, Switzerland), the stability of sample characteristics over the years allows trend observations. In France a few control questions reveal that only 30 percent of respondents are regular readers of *Gai Pied Hebdo*; a majority buys it only occasionally. Also, the Paris region is slightly over-represented, as also are small towns with no major cities nearby. The conclusion is that the readership over-represents two segments of the gay population: the most self-identifying ones living in the Paris region, the most isolated ones on the countryside. For them, occasional reading of a gay magazine seems to be the only relationship with a gay community.

Are snowball and quota samples less subject to bias? In Germany, Martin Dannecker from the University of Frankfurt recruited 903 respondents with a snowball system covering the whole national territory, almost the same size as Michael Bochow's newspaper sample of the same year (Dannecker, 1990). There were no significant differences between the two samples in age, residence, or education. However, the newspaper survey reached slightly more homosexuals with lower socioeconomic status (Bochow, 1990b). In France, face to face interview surveys using quota samples were conducted in 1986 and 1987. The aim of using the same questionnaire as the one enclosed in the newspaper was to measure the bias of readers of the gay press. Lower socioeconomic and educational status were obviously better represented in these quota samples of 300 respondents each. No statistically significant differences were found for most questions, except for the time of first behavior, which changes from two to six months earlier among readers of the gay press (Pollak, 1987).

For their sexual diary approach, project SIGMA recruited through gay newspapers. Recruitment results with ethnic groups and blue collar were disappointing. Out of a total of 273 diaries, 188 were returned, of which 125 (46 percent) identified themselves and 63 (23 percent) were unidentifiable. Of these, 107 (39 percent of the original total) said they were willing to continue to cooperate with the project, either by being interviewed or by doing further diaries (Coxon et al., 1990).

More qualitative research using anthropological and life history methodologies has been performed, either in combination with surveys or separately. Although based on fewer case observations (mostly less than 100 by project), such research was able to better understand psychological barriers to safer sex, in particular in younger populations and in the case of men having sex with men but not identifying themselves as being gay (Prieur, 1988).

After comparing these sampling methods, one can conclude:

- Accessing men having sex with men with low economic and educational status is extremely difficult. None of the sampling methods presented above has completely solved this problem.
- A major problem of cohort studies and of the sexual diary approach is the potential loss of participants over time. They do

have the advantage of being able to describe aggregate individual changes.

- As compared with snowball sampling or quota sampling, newspaper surveys have the advantage of a very short period of data collection. They are less time-consuming and involve fewer costs for administration and surveillance. For longitudinal observations, this short period is important as some changes (such as condom use) are very rapid, and data collection periods of several months can bring about biases in the interpretation.
- Besides differences in recruitment of respondents, the approaches discussed above have implications for the kind of questions which can be addressed, for the precision of data and their validity.

THE QUALITY OF DATA

Before 1984/85 only a few cohort studies used prevalence of anti-HIV as the dependent variable, because no relevant serologic tests were available. Because of the use of different dependent variables, the results of the various cohort studies are difficult to compare. Nearly all cohort studies try to establish a hierarchy between the different risk practices and modes of transmission. Because many techniques are often practiced in combination, it is difficult to determine the separate role of each sexual technique in the transmission of HIV. Later, regularity of safer sex in relation to HIV incidence became a major theme analyzed in cohort studies. The "cohort bias" does not allow one to draw generalizations. Clinic-based cohort studies usually show higher seroprevalence and higher levels of behavior changes than more representative approaches. In fact, cohort participants agreeing to regularly undergo the test have particularly high risk consciousness and very high levels of safer sex compliance. Therefore, the obvious advantage of the direct observation of HIV status as a dependent variable is counterweighted by other biases and difficulties when it comes to assessing behavior changes and compliance to safer sex.

Most of the research approaches on gay behavior rely on precoded self-administration questionnaires (newspaper surveys, snowball sampling). The space limitation for questionnaires included in newspapers usually allows not more than 100-130 questions to be asked. Questionnaires distributed in a snowball system, either in meeting places or sent by associations to their members, can be much longer and ask more detailed questions. Face-to-face interviewing is sometimes used in cohort studies and quota surveys.

Because of the impossibility of accurately recalling details of sexual behavior over longer periods, the sexual diary approach was developed. Diaries are kept by respondents on a daily basis. They complete them directly after sexual interactions (solitary, with one or more partners). This method provides greater accuracy in observations of patterns of sexual interactions and acts.

The accuracy of self-reported data was not only called into question for answers concerning sexuality, but also for the test and its results. These criticisms seem of lesser importance today after the analysis of self-reported data in several countries. To assess the quality of the gathered data, one may resort to various validation strategies. Internal coherence of the answers given by each respondent, interregional and international comparisons, and replication surveys repeated over short periods of time at least allow the researcher to evaluate the plausibility of the findings. In this respect, the data under discussion here are of good quality. At the same time, we observe that the interpretations of the data from the diary approach are coherent with the ones found in surveys. The results of the two approaches confirm each other.

As for trend observations derived from identical questionnaires repeated over periods of time, they are not "real" panel studies and do not offer analysis of behavior change patterns, possible only if one can follow individuals. In such replication surveys, the trends are general at a high level of aggregation. Also, each year, new respondents enter while others leave the sample. Over a period of five years, one can almost speak about a new "generation" that has entered the sample. For example, the "young" observed in a survey of 1985 are not the same generation as the young in a survey of 1990 who entered sexual life in a climate in which HIV risks are much more important than for their counterparts observed five years earlier. This must be taken into consideration in trend interpretations.

BEHAVIOR CHANGES

The different cohort studies have made it possible to trace the beginning of the epidemic in the Netherlands (van Griensven, 1989) and Denmark (Melbye, 1989) and, indirectly, in Western Europe. Retrospective blood analysis of the Danish cohort (nine percent infected in 1981) indicates that the first outbreak was "imported" from the United States, giving birth to a local epidemic with 26 percent of the cohort infected in 1984, 30 percent in 1987, and only one more in 1989. The Amsterdam cohort shows very similar results, with 31 percent infected in 1986, no new infections in 1987 and 1988, and three new infections in 1989.

All cohort studies agree that unprotected anal receptive practices are the most significant predictor of infection. But infection is also documented in the case of anogenital insertive practices. Oral sex with or without ejaculation in the mouth is still a controversial issue in the expert debate. When measuring behavior changes and compliance to safer sex, most surveys take unprotected anal penetration, including irregular condom use, as the most significant risk practice. Its absence in the sexual habits of a person and regular condom use are then considered, in statistical analysis, as indication for being in a safe zone.

Today, changes in sexual behavior based on informed choice are an integral part of the response of gay men to AIDS. From as early as 1985, all surveys show a very high degree of information and knowledge about HIV transmission. But behavior changes took much longer to be massively implemented.

Different patterns of change emerge from the surveys. Martin Dannecker's 1971 and 1987 surveys depict behavior changes over a longer period of time. They show that the number of sexual partners in the year before the investigation dropped substantially. A comparison in the United Kingdom between 1985 and 1988 and in France between 1985 and 1989 shows similar trends. This reduction in the number of sexual partners seems not to continue after 1988, according to the French yearly surveys and the German replication surveys of 1988 (Table 7).

The cross country comparison shows very similar changes in bonding patterns: around 50 percent of male homo- and bisexual survey respondents have a steady relationship, around half of the men

TABLE 7. Number of partners.

	Number of partners the last year (%)							Last 6 months (%)		Last 3 months (%)	
	1971:D[1]	1987:D[2]	1987:D[3]	1988:D[3]	1985:UK[4]	1988:UK[4]	1989:I[5]	1985:F[6]	1990:F[6]	1987:CH[7]	1990:CH[8]
None	—	2	4	4	6	2	10	5	8	10	8
1	6	15	17	16	31	51	—	16	26	26	26
2-5	19	33	36	37	—	—	48	31	32	37	37
6-10	17	18	16	15	—	—	—	21	18	18	18
11-20	23	13	12	14	51	34	—	17	10	—	—
21-50	20	12	11	10	—	—	35	—	—	8	10
51-100	9	5	3	3	9	5	—	10	6	—	—
More	6	2	1	1	3	8	6	—	—	—	—
	100	100	100	100	100	100	100	100	100	100	100
	(N=789)	(N=903)	(N=924)	(n=1122)	(n=1256)	(n=1300)	(n=1340)	(n=1000)	(n=2000)	(n=795)	(n=720)

1. M. Dannecker, R. Reiche
2. M. Dannecker
3. M. Bochow
4. McManus, McEvoy
5. Only casual partners; H. Sasse et al.
6. M. Pollak
7. F. Dubois-Arber
8. J. B. Masur

having such a relationship have sex exclusively with this steady partner (Germany, France, Switzerland, United Kingdom). In France, the overall number of steady relationships has remained unchanged from 1985 to 1990, while the number of closed couple relationships has increased from ten percent to 25 percent. Due to the risk of infection, there is a tendency to even limit sexual interaction with the main steady partner and in closed couple relationships. In several countries (France, Germany), around 20 percent of respondents, who earlier frequented these places, avoid bathhouses and saunas. In Italy, the 1989 survey shows ten percent living in an exclusive couple relationship and 75 percent having stable and occasional sexual partners.

The same surveys show a drastic reduction in the frequency of anal penetration and, if maintained, an increase in condom use. According to Martin Dannecker, only mutual masturbation and body rubbing (frottage) have been maintained at similar levels as in the early 1970s. All practices involving body fluids (anal and oral), including deep kissing, have been sharply reduced (Dannecker, 1990). This observation is substantiated in other research. Project SIGMA also shows that masturbation is the most frequently practiced sexual act (Coxon, Davies, and McManus, 1990).

Table 8 shows the frequency distribution of different practices in France and Germany in 1988. A very similar pattern emerges from these figures.

We observe similar figures in Italy, although the relative frequency was not asked. With casual partners, 77 percent practice mutual masturbation, 78 percent orogenital receptive, 76 percent orogenital insertive, 52 percent anogenital receptive, and 64 percent anogenital insertive sex (Sasse et al., 1990).

In all countries under observation, condom use has significantly increased in the last decade. In Denmark, a survey in the western branches of LBL showed that condom use increased from three percent in the early 1980s to 82 percent (regular and irregular) in 1987 (Bottzauw, Hermansen, and Tauris, 1989b). In France, condom use increased from five percent in 1985 to 74 percent in 1990, with 49 percent using condoms regularly. The Italian survey demonstrates a link between condom use and all orogenital and anogenital sexual practices and to different types of partners. Tables 9 and 10

TABLE 8. Frequency distribution of sexual practices.

	Always F[1]	Always G[2]	Often F	Often G	Sometimes F	Sometimes G	Never F	Never G
Masturbation								
Solitary	45%	25%	44%	49%	10%	23%	1%	1%
Mutual	—	15%	—	38%	—	39%	—	6%
Orogenital								
Insertive	22%	15%	47%	33%	22%	43%	9%	8%
Receptive	24%	16%	45%	30%	22%	41%	3%	10%
Anogenital								
Insertive	10%	5%	28%	14%	34%	48%	28%	29%
Receptive	10%	5%	25%	13%	31%	44%	24%	34%

1. M. Pollak, 1989.
2. M. Bochow, 1989.

show that condoms are not very often used for oral sex. Condom use with steady partners is significantly lower than with casual partners.

The French yearly surveys relate the amount and the speed of these changes to relatively homogenous subgroups observed since 1985 (Pollak, 1988b):

1. Homosexuals living in localities of less than 20,000 inhabitants, often hiding their sexual preference, and whose homosexuality is not accepted by family and colleagues, feared social discrimination as much if not more than being contaminated. Lack of solidarity with a "gay group and destiny" was widespread; capacity for individual behavior changes was limited, and diffusion of condom use was slow before 1987; propensity for repressive measures was high (compulsory testing, quarantining). The feeling of being unable to protect themselves with adequate behavior changes explains this demand

for state intervention, that rapidly decreased, even in this sub-group, as condom use became more widespread.

2. Blue collar gays barely felt concerned by AIDS in 1985. Only after 1987 did they recognize the risk and start to change sexual behavior.

3. Lower middle-class gays in big cities (service sector) showed the highest degree of denial. Although well-informed about the disease, they often presented the "risk group" classification as an attempt to discriminate against them. Their biographical background, including breaking up with their family because of their being gay, explains their ambivalent reactions in the early days of the epidemic. Only in 1986 did they start to rapidly change their behavior.

4. Higher middle classes, in particular intellectual professionals, were the first to adapt quickly to the risk of HIV transmission by giving up anal intercourse or by using condoms. They were also the first to know HIV carriers in their personal environment. The first voluntary associations recruited their first members and volunteers from among them.

5. Before 1986, skepticism prevailed among young homosexuals below age 25. They identified AIDS as a disease of their parent's generation and resented the labeling of the "young" as a specifically exposed group. After 1986, differences appear in this age group: students follow the model of the higher middle classes, the others that of blue collars.

As shown by this longitudinal approach, safer sex is a culturally differentiated process. It does not result from individual rational choices. Sex is a social activity, an interaction subject to negotiation. Therefore, adoption of safer sex is a process of progressive changes. It starts with easily implemented modifications before integrating more difficult ones. One can classify sexual behavior changes in two broad categories: selection strategies and protection strategies.

Selection strategies include all attempts to avoid people (less partners, not engaging in sex with people because of their look, their age or geographic origin), places (no more saunas and backrooms), and situations (no alcohol or drug consumption) considered risky or which might reduce self control.

TABLE 9. Regular and/or irregular condom use according to practices and type of partners (Italy, 1989).

	Insertive anogenital	Receptive anogenital	Insertive orogenital	Receptive orogenital
Steady partners	62%	44%	19%	20%
Steady and casual partners	78%	68%	33%	28%
Only casual partners	69%	61%	33%	26%

Source: Sasse, 1990. These high figures change if one considers the frequency of condom use.

Protection strategies consist of modifying the sexual acts themselves. This involves changing the frequency distribution of the sexual repertory from anogenital toward orogenital and masturbation activities, and using protection instruments such as condoms.

In the process of adopting safer sex behavior the relative share of selection and protection strategies changes over time. In the early days of the epidemic, changes were almost exclusively concerned with more cautious selection of partners and places. These choices were based on personal appreciations of risk, often badly informed and incoherent. One remembers sentences such as: "Avoid American tourists," "don't fuck with big city gays," etc. They had relatively little effect on the progression of the infection. Only in the mid-1980s when the size of the epidemic became visible to all male homo- and bisexuals, did they start to protect themselves during the sexual act, in particular with condoms. The widespread use of the HIV antibody test allows people to conceive selection strategies no longer on "guesses" but on knowledge of the serostatus of oneself and potential sexual partners. Therefore we observe, after 1988/89, new changes in safer sex adoption with the rising importance of mixed strategies and differentiated risk taking such as no precautions with a steady partner in the case of a common seronegativity, safer sex and condoms with all casual partners (Table 11).

TABLE 10. Frequency of condom use according to practices and type of partners.

	Condom Use		
	Always	Sometimes	Never
Insertive anogenital with			
–stable partners	25%	24%	51%
–casual partners	42%	36%	22%
Receptive anogenital with			
–stable partners	27%	23%	50%
–casual partners	48%	32%	20%
Insertive orogenital with			
–stable partners	3%	9%	88%
–casual partners	7%	24%	69%
Receptive orogenital with			
–stable partners	2%	9%	89%
–casual partners	5%	21%	74%

Source: Sasse, 1990.

It is extremely difficult to compare this major swing to safer sex in a cross-national perspective because of differences in question formulation and in the periods of data collection. We have chosen the surveys undertaken between 1987 and 1990 as years with the most comparable data.

One observes a few striking differences between national patterns which can, in part, be explained by differences in the official arguments used in prevention campaigns. In Germany, France, and Ireland regular condom use in anal penetration is becoming a gay habit. In Switzerland and, even more so, in the Netherlands, male homo- and bisexuals have massively abandoned anal penetration. Despite these impressive behavior changes, one observes, at the end of the 1980s, levels of unprotected anal sex of more than 20 percent, going up to 29 percent in France and 39 percent in the Netherlands. These figures indicate people who practice unprotected and/or protected

TABLE 11. Patterns of behavior changes in France.

	1985	1990
Strategies of selection	30%	10%
Mixed strategies	5%	58%
Strategies of protection	—	19%

Selection: Avoidance of certain types of partners and meeting places.

Protection: No anal intercourse, regular use of condoms.

Source: Pollak, Schiltz, 1991.

anogenital sex. Therefore they are maximum estimates which include monogamous couples and people protecting themselves with anonymous partners and taking no precautions with steady partners- whose HIV status they probably know (Table 12).

The insistence on the limited safety of condoms before the development of a special anal condom in the Netherlands might have had the effect of creating an attitude of "condom skepticism" and of maintenance of non-protection for those who could not renounce anal sex. Together with the very explicit anti-test policy, this might explain the relatively bad prevention results in the Netherlands. The Danish newspaper survey of 1988 (2,100 respondents) did not survey behavior change, but 33 percent of respondents indicated at least one unprotected anal intercourse in the past year with a partner with either discordant or unknown HIV-status.

The type of relationship is the most important predictor of unprotected anal sex (Project SIGMA, 1990). All surveys show that, today, unprotected anal penetration is still found mostly in closed couple relationships. The smallest ratio of those practicing unprotected anal penetration occurs with men in a steady, but not sexually exclusive, relationship. The regular use of a condom during anal intercourse by gay men with no steady relationship is relatively unaffected by the number of times they practice it and the number of partners (Bochow, 1990b).

Since 1988 and 1989, there seems to be a slowdown of further

TABLE 12. Safer sex practices: A cross-national comparison.

	Switzerland[1] 1987	Switzerland[1] 1990	Germany[2] 1988	France[3] 1988	France[3] 1990	Netherlands[4] 1988	Ireland[5] 1988	Italy[6] 1989(rec)	Italy[6] 1989(ins)
Do not practice anal penetration	50%	42%	18%	24%	30%	45%	27%	48%	36%
Regular condom use for anal penetration	30%	34%	48%	47%	49%	16%	47%	24%	29%
Practice nonprotected anal penetration	20%	23%	34%	29%	21%	39%	26%	28%	45%
	100%	100%	100%	100%	100%	100%	100%	100%	100%

1. F. Dubois-Arber, J. B. Masur (figures for the last three months)
2. M. Bochow (figures for the last 12 months)
3. M. Pollak (figures for the last six months)
4. R. Tielman (figures for the last six months)
5. Gay Health Action (figures for the last 12 months)
6. H. Sasse (figures for the last 12 months with casual partners, separately for receptive and insertive anal penetration)

reduction of unprotected anal sex. Project SIGMA reports a shift away from safer sex in the United Kingdom, largely due to an increase in the number of men with regular partners. The same is observed for Germany and France. If we take this element into account, the proportion of gay men still engaging in unsafe sex with casual partners of unknown serostatus is in the ten percent range in these three countries. Also, the regular use of condoms allows many gay men to restart anal sex that they had avoided in previous years.

We can conclude:

- On the most general level, we observe the swing in the sexual repertory from anogenital and orogenital practices to solitary and mutual masturbation,
- the reduction in the number of sexual partners, the increase in closed couple relationships,
- the widespread diffusion of condom use, becoming increasingly regular,
- the adoption of different sexual approaches to steady and casual partners.

YOUNG MEN HAVING SEX WITH MEN

A specific question often addressed is teenage sexuality and the risks involved during the "coming out" period. Often research projects presented in international AIDS conferences define "youth" from 18 to 30 years. Here we are concerned with gay men below the age of 20. No major research project was devoted exclusively to this age group. But KABP surveys of more than one thousand respondents offer sufficiently large subsamples for statistical analysis. In project SIGMA there were 111 respondents under 21, 60 in the 1990 French survey and 135 in the Italian survey of 1989 were less than 20 years old.

The average age of the first sexual encounter is between 15 and 17 years. In France, this age increased by one year between 1986 and 1990. The proportion of gays under 21 practicing anal intercourse (receptive rather than insertive) is lower than in older groups: around 40 percent. Young gay men, having grown in a more tolerant climate than the older generations, tend to engage more often in closed couple relationships and are likely to use condoms for anal intercourse if practiced. After a period of hesitation, the youngest generation, raised in a climate of AIDS, is becoming a "safer sex" generation, showing the most regular condom use (Davies et al., 1991).

Despite a more tolerant climate, "coming out" is still a complicated process. One could interpret the passive part played most of the time in anal intercourse by young men as revealing that they are operating within a set of expectations about sexual techniques that relies on stereotyped heterosexual preconceptions.

Bisexual contacts, much more frequent below the age of 25 than later, is another example pointing to the difficulties of entering gay life. Although 80 percent of the respondents in the French survey of 1990 indicate that they became conscious of their sexual preference for men some three years before they first started their sexual career, many have their first sexual experience with women.

BISEXUALITY

Twenty to 40 percent of the different samples composed of gay men have had periods of experiences with women, often before age 25 (Pollak and Schiltz, 1991; Weatherburn et al., 1990). In Italy 34 percent of respondents reported sexual contacts with men and women at the moment of survey. This high figure can be attributed to the young age of the sample, with 40 percent of respondents aged 25 years and younger.

In Germany, France, and Switzerland, the proportion of respondents with male and female partners at the time of survey is in the ten-20 percent range. The number of female partners is rarely above five. Most bisexual respondents have only one female partner and many more male partners. This is not surprising, as most practicing bisexual men are married or divorced. Married men usually have less male partners than divorced ones. In terms of sexual practices, bisexuals tend to protect themselves against the risk of HIV transmission with their male partners. Very rarely do married men use condoms for vaginal penetration with their wife. These differences correspond to the ones already observed when comparing steady and casual homosexual partners.

Bisexuality is a minority phenomenon, but many gay men go through bisexual or heterosexual phases. Therefore bisexuality has to be more deeply analyzed, as it plays an important role in HIV transmission from the homo- into the heterosexual population.

DETERMINANTS FOR BEHAVIOR CHANGES

Most empirical studies on factors relating to sexual behavior change among male homo- and bisexuals began after substantial change had occurred, and thus provide greater insight into the reasons for sexual change among later rather than early adopters of safer sex (Cohen and Couturier, 1990). Among the different factors discussed are the amount of information, attitudes and beliefs about transmission, perceived personal risk exposure, social proximity to AIDS and seropositive friends, socioeconomic status and age, types of relationships, self-identity and self-esteem (in particular with respect to one's being gay), and the test and its results (Cohen, 1989; Coates, Stall, and Hoffi, 1988). The influence of the type of relationship and the test have been discussed above.

Information and accurate knowledge about the risk are necessary preconditions for perceived need for personal change and the change itself, but information in itself is not sufficient for explaining change. Social proximity to infected people induces the feeling of personal risk exposure and low-risk behaviors. This is reinforced by the extent of social integration in a network of supportive groups, and by the degree to which one's social environment accepts homosexuality. The same dimension is often approached in a psychological fashion under the concepts of "self-identity" and "self-esteem."

For more isolated men who have sex with men, or for young men struggling with their gay identity, the desire to experience and to fulfill a sexual need can overwhelm known dangers of unsafe sex. These situational and personality factors have been put forward in qualitative research using in-depth interviewing (Prieur, 1988, 1990). Even in later stages of the epidemic, men knowledgeable about the risks of unsafe sex continue this practice. For some, there is a need for intimacy, and they feel that unsafe sex is the best way to give and receive love. Another reason for continuing unsafe practices is fatalism and a sense of there being no future.

Longitudinal observations also point to the change of correlations among these different factors in time as the epidemic progresses.

The French sociological trend observations show three phases in the process of change:

Phase 1: before 1985-1986: emergence of "pioneers" practicing new sexual behaviors from among those who were the first to know people affected by the disease personally. To this proximity, one must add factors reinforcing the predispositions and capacities to change: self-esteem and the feeling of being socially accepted; confidence in medical authorities and concern with health. Although the approach of these safer sex pioneers looks like the result of an individual rational "decision," it is overdetermined by their middle class status and high educational level.

Phase 2: 1986-1988: With the more widespread use of the test, the epidemic becomes "visible." Particularly inside concerned groups, such as the gay community, there emerges a feeling of identification with a collective risk and new positive ethics of sexual precaution, which goes beyond people who know infected persons personally. Rapid diffusion of behavior changes in all middle classes is favored by this new sexual ethic and the identification with a gay destiny and a community. This phase was initiated and promoted by voluntary associations while the government campaign came later, reinforcing the already engaged swing.

Phase 3: after 1988: After a process of rapid diffusion of sexual behavior changes, one observes its limits, which are of a macrosocial nature. The factors usually perceived as being at the origin of cumulative socioeconomic handicaps and inequalities also limit risk adequate behaviors: low socioeconomic status and fragility (such as unemployment), lack of confidence in the future, low educational level. In these cases personal counseling is of particular importance. These empirical observations also suggest that one has to differentiate between various levels of factors that favor or hinder sexual behavior change induced by the risk of HIV infection:

- individual predispositions,
- factors of the immediate environment (community specific),
- macrosocietal determinants.

Part Three:
Concluding Remarks

EPIDEMIOLOGICAL BACKGROUND

National statistics on HIV infection and AIDS are difficult to compare. Some national systems of data collection are based on voluntary, others on compulsory reporting. Some collect information on HIV infections (reporting positive HIV antibody test results), others on fully diagnosed AIDS cases. In the absence, for ethical and economic reasons, of systematic testing programs, HIV-seroprevalence estimates rely on diverse sources: blood donors, STD clinics, laboratories, hospitals, etc. They are subject to bias.

On the European level, the European Center for Epidemiological Monitoring of AIDS collects, analyzes, and compares data reported by 32 European countries (European Center for Epidemiological Monitoring of AIDS, 1990). These are the best available data for describing the epidemic and its spread from one segment of the population to another.

Table 13 depicts a generally lower proportion of HIV+ homo- and bisexual men, in 1990, than in 1985. With more than 70 percent testing positive, the epidemic is still primarily concentrated in this group in the United Kingdom, Germany, the Netherlands, and the Scandinavian countries. In southern Europe (Italy, Spain) IVDUs predominate. In Portugal, Greece, France, and Austria, there are some 50 percent male homo- and bisexual cases compared with 20-30 percent of IVDUs. Heterosexual transmission is widespread in Belgium, particularly among Africans living there or seeking treatment. If one only counts cases among Belgian citizens, the proportion of male homo- and bisexual cases increases to 55 percent.

According to a WHO analysis, recent annual growth rates for Europe are lower in the homo/bisexual transmission group than

TABLE 13. Epidemiological background data.

	Cumulated rate per million		percent of homo-bisexual cases	
	Total population	Homo-bisexual cases	1985	1990
Austria	66	29	65%	44%
Belgium	83	30	20%*	36%*
Denmark	140	106	90%	76%
Finland	15	9	80%	81%
France	234	124	60%	53%
Germany F.R.	71	50	75%	70%
Greece	41	21	—	50%
Ireland	52	20	77%	39%
Italy	143	22	24%	15%
Luxembourg	70	42	—	58%
Netherlands	103	83	81%	80%
Norway	46	31	26%	17%
Portugal	56	26	67%	57%
Spain	193	31	26%	17%
Sweden	60	43	80%	72%
Switzerland	243	109	62%	46%
United Kingdom	72	57	93%	80%

*These low figures can be explained by the high proportion of African cases in the Belgian statistics (see p. 73).

among IVDUs (48 percent of newly reported cases versus 82 percent). Nevertheless, the fact that homo- and bisexual cases show a slower progression than IVDUs does not justify the hypothesis that there has been a significant improvement in the situation in the first group, but only demonstrates the different phases of the epidemic, with IVDUs entering into the picture later than male homo- and bisexuals.

At the moment, the AIDS surveillance statistics do not allow us to interpret the present situation in terms of new incidence. The uncertainties (incubation period, etc.) are just too great. A simple statistical analysis can help us to detect a few trends, however.

In a few countries, the proportion of male homo- and bisexual AIDS cases hardly changed between 1985 and 1990 (Finland, Germany, Netherlands). In most countries, this proportion has decreased less than ten percent in this period: France (–7 percent), Germany (–5 percent), Italy (–9 percent), Spain (–9 percent), Sweden (–8 percent), and Portugal (–10 percent). In the other West European countries the proportion of male homo- and bisexual cases dropped more than ten percent to a little more than 20 percent: Austria (–21 percent), Denmark (–14 percent), Ireland (–38 percent), Norway (–21 percent), Switzerland (–16 percent), and the United Kingdom (–13 percent).

Per se, these first figures do not reveal very much, for the base line situation differs significantly from country to country, as shown in Table 1. In particular, the lesser proportion of gay cases has to be put in perspective with respect to the overall epidemic development. If one looks at the histograms country by country, it becomes clear that there has not been a slowdown of the epidemic in the homo- and bisexual population.

J. W. Duyvendak and R. Koopmans (1991) propose a sophisticated statistical analysis that will present a clearer picture. Between 1985 and 1990, the rank order of homo- and bisexual cases per million inhabitants hardly changed among West European countries: In 1990, France has taken over first place from Switzerland, which held it since 1986. The third column of Table 14 shows the increases during the period. Here the rank order is quite different.

In absolute numbers, the highest increases occurred in the countries where a high number of cases was already reached in the mid-1980s. However, the rank of a country in terms of the increase rate tells a different story. In most countries, the male homo- and bisexual cases have increased by 330 to 380 percent. A particularly high rate of progression, 1112 percent, is observed in Greece. Austria (607 percent), Portugal (537 percent), Italy (514 percent) show an important progression of the epidemic in the male homo- and bisexual population. With 400 and 436 percent respectively, France and the Netherlands also show increases clearly situated above the most common situation. With 277 and 308 percent, Switzerland and Sweden show the lowest rates of increase in their male homo- and bisexual cases.

TABLE 14. Increase of male homo- and bisexual cases. Rank order in 1986 and 1990.

	AIDS/mill. end of 1990	AIDS/mill. in 1986	% increase 1986-1990
1. France	124.1	24.8 (2)	400 (7)
2. Switzerland	109.3	29.0 (1)	277 (14)
3. Denmark	106.3	23.7 (3)	349 (11)
4. Netherlands	82.5	15.5 (4)	436 (6)
5. United Kingdom	54.9	12.5 (5)	339 (12)
6. Germany F.R.	50.0	10.7 (6)	367 (10)
7. Sweden	43.2	10.6 (7)	308 (13)
8. Norway	30.9	6.6 (8)	368 (9)
9. Spain	29.7	3.7 (11)	703 (2)
10. Belgium	29.8	6.2 (9)	381 (8)
11. Austria	29.0	4.1 (10)	607 (3)
12. Portugal	24.2	3.8 (12)	537 (4)
13. Italy	21.5	3.5 (13)	514 (5)
14. Greece	20.6	1.7 (14)	1112 (1)

This analysis of Duyvendak and Koopmans (1991) suggests that prevention makes the difference. The Mediterranean South, Austria, Portugal, and Ireland but also the Netherlands and France have a comparatively bad prevention record.

This report will try to give some explanations to these differences, with the hypothesis:

– prevention can make a difference,
– the later prevention starts and the higher the incidence rate at that moment, the more difficult it is to get under control.

SUCCESSES AND FAILURES OF PREVENTION IN WESTERN EUROPE

After these empirical and theoretical discussions, we can return to the problem of explaining country differences in prevention efficiency. In this section, we will look at the specific countries which did best (Switzerland, Sweden) and worst (Greece, Spain, Austria, Portugal). Two countries with relatively high increases in AIDS cases deserve special attention, as their rank does not correspond to what is generally believed about their prevention efforts: the Netherlands and France.

We have stressed several elements in this report. Time is a major resource in the fight against an epidemic. To be efficient, prevention must start early, before a large pool of infected people develops. Even if spectacular and highly visible, punctual actions have less long-term efficiency than continuous uninterrupted efforts. Arguments should be explicit, clear, and outspoken about sexuality and condom use.

The organizational conditions in which prevention takes place are crucial. The intermediary organizational level between the most exposed groups and public authorities is essential to spread the message and maintain a climate of confidence and trust. Therefore, network density and organizational continuity is essential for voluntary associations and NGOs. Another important point is the coordination with public health authorities responsible for large public education campaigns.

Let us first address the two European countries with the best prevention results. In Switzerland, preventive action did not begin much earlier than in most other countries, but when it got off the ground, voluntary and public actions were well coordinated and conceived. This was facilitated by the predominant role of a major AIDS organization closely related to the gay community. Multimedia campaigns in the written press, TV, and radio were combined with targeted community-based actions.

The situation in Sweden is quite different. Here the very early start of preventive action is the merit of gay organizations. Public authorities became active in 1985, as in many other European countries. They chose to deal with AIDS according to their traditional public health approach. This approach, used in STD control, combines technical elements such as testing with coercive measures (partner tracing, quarantining) and public information and education campaigns. The coercive part of the program fueled tension and conflict between the voluntary and the public sector, but the high degree of public confidence in the state has enabled people to overcome these tensions as gay organizations no longer feared that testing and partner tracing might be used against them. Their cooperation on the local level with health administrators has guaranteed preventive efficiency and avoided stigmatization and discrimination, despite the importance given to repressive elements in the official policy.

The situation in the Mediterranean South reads like a contrast program. Public action in Greece has been limited to a TV campaign. The intermediary sector hardly exists. With its important tourist sector, the absence of prevention in this country had a dramatic effect. In Portugal, public action has been more intensive, with annual leaflet and TV campaigns. But here, too, no community-based gay organizations exist that might play a mediation role in prevention. In Italy and Spain, extreme fragmentation of the voluntary sector has hindered more efficient action. Public campaigns were delivered without continuity; periods of intense activism were followed by long periods of inactivity.

The poor prevention results in Austria require special attention. Actions by a gay organization and the government started in 1983, the year the first AIDS cases were diagnosed in the country. On the formal level, Austria's AIDS policy is based on the same model as those of Germany and Switzerland. A large AIDS organization, subsidized to almost 100 percent by government, acts in close coordination with health authorities. Despite its important gay constituency, the Austria AIDS organization, with its anonymous testing centers, is very biomedically oriented. Unlike the Swiss and German campaigns, the Austrian's were much less sexually explicit. The themes developed were solidarity and compassion rather than condoms. High conservative officials of the Catholic Church condemned homosexuals and condoms. Although not openly intervening in the policy debates, the lobbying power of the Catholic Church, to which almost 90 percent of Austrians belong, might have had an adverse effect on condom promotion. In contrast, the gay community is much too weak for lobbying and defending its interest.

In general, one observes a difference between countries of Protestant and of Catholic traditions, where massive condom promotion posed more problems and used ambiguous terms and images in order to avoid controversy, less with a population open to health arguments than with a powerful church bureaucracy.

Two other countries with bad prevention results, though for very different reasons, demonstrate how intertwined political and cultural traditions in the health sector and in the gay community are when it comes to fighting AIDS. The paradox is that the relatively bad prevention results for male homo- and bisexuals in both countries might be explained by the weakness of the gay community in France and by its strength in the Netherlands (Duyvendak and Koopmans, 1991). In fact, preventive action by both associations and government started late in France. Despite the predominant role of AIDES, a very respectable organization well-introduced in the medical world, the government did not support it in any way comparable to how similar groups were assisted in Germany or Switzerland. Also, the French discovery of the virus opened exaggerated hopes. As a consequence, a biomedical approach took precedence over prevention.

Gay representatives in the Netherlands participated in decision making from the very beginning. One could almost say that they shaped the Dutch prevention philosophy. Community action was stressed, for out of the tradition of fighting discrimination and homophobia, the Dutch struggle against AIDS was largely defined as a fight against stigmatization. It is a paradox that this theme was most developed in the Netherlands, a country proud of its openness, legal provisions, and satisfactory status of gay people in society. A rigid anti-test ideology and the officially reinforced condom skepticism are additional elements of the Dutch prevention philosophy which might have had negative consequences. The time spent waiting for the special Dutch anal condom for men might be responsible for periods of infection in the early days of the epidemic. In France, national pride concerning biomedical research had detrimental effects. One could say that Dutch national gay pride concerning special products and services for gay men precluded a pragmatic approach in favor of using protection instruments already available.

In the countries not specifically discussed here, the mix of information and education instruments has produced relatively similar outcomes, as shown in our discussion of the epidemiological situation at the beginning of this text.

After years of "safer sex learning," one can formulate an optimistic or a pessimistic prediction for the near future:

- The optimistic prediction reads: a new level of sexual behavior and sexual activity could be reached, one that takes into account the risks involved, one in which adequate coping strategies are integrated in such a way that further urgent need for change in sexual behavior would be rendered superfluous.
- The pessimistic prediction reads: after a few years of important behavior changes and regularity in condom use, and in a climate with fewer primary prevention campaigns, people "forget," causing increased incidence rates after a slow down of the epidemic among men having sex with men.

The optimistic hypothesis will largely depend on continued prevention efforts in the community and in society at large. The pessimistic hypothesis is favored by lower investment in prevention, public guesses about a leveling-off of the epidemic and lower levels of personal concern and risk awareness.

To monitor these changes, nationally and on the European level, comparable questionnaire instruments should be developed, usable for newspaper and snowball self-administered surveys. To access the male homo- and bisexual population, the channels used should be adapted to local realities. Such surveys should be replicated every two or three years.

AIDS PREVENTION
AND THE HEALTH BELIEF MODEL

Many characteristics of HIV infection create specific difficulties for traditional behavioral models:

- the nature and complexity of the threat presented by AIDS is extreme and extends to one's most intimate relationships;
- extreme uncertainty characterizes the entire process from exposure through infection to diagnosis;
- the social context creates risks of stigmatization of HIV carriers and persons with AIDS.

It is also obvious that rapid changes in human behavior are occurring because of the threat of AIDS. Traditional epidemiological risk factors and socio-cultural variables do not seem totally adequate for the understanding of differences of patterns of change in sexual behavior.

Adaptation of sexual behavior to the risk of HIV infection is very rapid in the most exposed segment of the population, men having sex with men, and unequally distributed according to proximity to the disease, social class, age and education. Therefore only longitudinal research starting at an early moment of the process aids understanding of the whole cycle, as well as group-specific forms and rates of patterns of change. This necessity is emphasized by the evolution of the epidemic itself: while the number of penetrative sexual partners is the main predictor of infection when incidence rate is low, this is not the case when incidence increases, as is shown by data from studies among American homosexual men (Kingsley et al., 1987).

Finally, control of HIV transmission requires that changes in behavior be applied consistently in time and in all types of situations. Factors which contribute to initiating behavioral change are not necessarily the same as those that would favor a persistent change, and instability in behavioral risk reduction has often been observed.

Consensus will be easily reached among social scientists about some general conclusions that emerged from the literature on behavioral risk modifications, especially through health information and education, which have already been confirmed by studies on AIDS, including the surveys under review:

1. There is no direct relationship between an individual's knowledge of and attitudes toward a disease and behavior. Information alone is therefore insufficient to promote meaningful changes in risk behavior. Illustrations of this point are numerous in studies about different health related problems such as tobacco consumption, drug and alcohol abuse patterns, obesity, etc. In the field of sexual behavior, one can refer to research on the impact of programs to prevent teenage pregnancy. While information on birth control significantly

increases knowledge about contraception, likelihood of pregnancy and sexual activity are not consequently affected (Lance, 1975).

Because sex is a powerful motive and because sexual practices are maintained by past experiences, immediacy of gratification, reinforcement by fantasies, and often interpersonal influence or even coercion, it can be expected that sexual activities are especially difficult to change through information provision alone. One can easily agree with Nelkin (Nelkin, 1987) that the common examples of direct behavioral responses to information are "all in areas in which alternative choices are available so that changes in behavior require no significant changes in life-style." All studies among homosexual/bisexual men have confirmed that individual knowledge about AIDS risk is not statistically related to reported frequency of high-risk sexual practices for HIV infection or to observed behavioral change to lower exposure (Kelly and St. Lawrence, 1988).

2. Research on behavioral change has repeatedly revealed that trust and credibility in the source of information and social reinforcement by peers within the community are necessary conditions for effective intervention. Early findings of experimental social psychology on "small group decisions" have emphasized the importance of adaptation to ambiguity or change in the environment through interpersonal communication, and referred to mechanisms such as group polarization and group pressure, social confirmation, norm formation and minority innovation (Bandura, 1969; Sherif, 1935). In one of the largest American cohort studies of homosexual/bisexual men, supportive peer norms appeared to be the only factor related to longitudinal behavioral change for risk reduction of HIV sexual transmission (Emmons et al., 1986).

However, when it comes to explanatory models for determinants of behavior, the main (implicit or explicit) reference of most AIDS studies remains the Health Belief Model (HBM) which was established in the context of assessment of health education programs for other diseases (with a special input from the internationally organized 10-year research project in North Karelia, Finland, on prevention of coronary heart disease) (Puska, Jissinen, and Tuanilheto, 1985; Jette et al., 1981; Janz and Becker, 1984). In its current formulation, the HBM assumes that the following factors mostly determine the likelihood that an individual will take a given preventive or curative action with regard to a particular health problem:

- the perceived individual susceptibility of the disease,
- the perceived seriousness of the disease,
- the perceived benefits of the health action,
- the perceived barriers to the health action,
- certain cues to action,
- modifying demographic and psycho-sociological factors (including so-called "general health motivation").

The combination of perceived high susceptibility to the illness and great perceived benefits of action usually appears as a good "predictor" of adoption of behavioral change; it is also often assumed (without experimental evidence) that the components of the model combine in a multiplicative manner to influence behavior. It does not seem unfair to consider the Health Belief Model as an attempt to build an operational application to health education of classical social psychological learning theories: the assumption is made that health beliefs are modifiable, especially through risk-education behavioral change.

It cannot be denied that valuable practical recommendations for health education have been derived from the Health Belief Model (or at least from empirical research referring to its conceptual framework): effective health/behavior-changing educational messages must include explicit information indicating that the severity of the potential illness is great, that the individual receiving the message is susceptible to the illness, that behavior change can be effected to reduce the likelihood of illness, and that the relative benefits of behavior change are greater than the costs (including psychological costs); effectiveness of the message is also increased when it simultaneously provides information on the specific behavior change needed to reduce risk, offers a cognitive rationale for why these changes produce practical reduction of risks, and provides positive encouragement for making health-related changes (Siegel, Grodsky, and Herman, 1986). If the importance of exhaustive and accurate information is commonly accepted, discussion is still open on the most effective content of messages, such as the role of fear in risk awareness (Job, 1988). While it is clear that prevention campaigns based only on fear are likely to prove ineffective and that individuals overwhelmed by fear are more likely to feel that risk exposure is inevitable, it is often argued that messages producing moderate levels of fear will facilitate behavioral change to the extent that they are completed by a positive and reassuring description of the consequence of change.

When it comes to the explanatory power of determinants of behavior from the Health Belief Model, however, many criticisms may be raised. Once it is no longer used for practical purposes (designing and evaluating health education programs), its explanatory power easily looks like a tautology.

In particular, it is obvious that the association between health beliefs and behavior is bidirectional, and that health beliefs are as much a consequence of behavior as its cause. So, it is always possible to find an *a posteriori* relationship between observed behavior change (or absence of change) and a general model of perceived risk/perceived benefit.

Collective influence on individual mechanisms of risk has also been noted by research on comparative estimation of different risks for health, especially in the field of technological risks (Fischhoff et al., 1982). Three characteristics maximize risk aversion: non-familiarity, catastrophic potential (simultaneous exposure in space and time of a higher number of individuals) and lack of control (Lefaure and Moatti, 1983). This last factor does not refer to the traditional distinction between voluntary (and therefore more acceptable) and involuntary risk, which has been proved to be invalid (Slovic, Fischhoff, and Lichtenstein, 1980), but rather to the individual feeling that the society or community as a whole is able to control the risk and its detrimental consequences.

Finally, at a societal macro-level, risk perceptions are heavily influenced by political, cultural, and social factors, such as membership in a social class or involvement in a social milieu. Attitudes toward risk are closely embedded in a system of beliefs, values, and ideals that constitute a culture (and subculture): thus, different cultures and social groups will emphasize certain risks and minimize others. Perceptions of risk are also closely connected to legitimizing moral principles (Douglas and Wildavsky, 1982). A judgment about risk can be a social comment, reflecting points of tension and value conflicts in a given society.

The previous considerations lead to the most fundamental criticisms of the Health Belief Model. In a way, this model is not different from the conventional axioms of expected utility theory which are based on the assumption of rational individuals acting as utility (or risk/benefit, cost/benefit ratio) maximizers.

Because it is centered on the individual, the HBM neglects the dynamic social interactions that shape behavior. Even on the individual level, it only takes into account cognitive elements and neglects other psychological determinants of the ability to cope in situations of risk. As some behavioral situations (notably competition or intergroup conflict, and perhaps affective/sexual relationships) engage social identity and identification with a particular group, research on sexual behavior and risk of HIV infection clearly implies a focus on the specific social interactions which influence individual behavior, largely absent in the HBM. In the case of HIV prevention, community mobilization and a social climate of tolerance and solidarity are major elements for maintaining risk awareness and adequate behaviors.

References

Algra, Y., O. Bergès, G. Pelé, M. Pollak. "New Sexual Behavior Among Gay Men in Europe: Evaluation of the Role of 'jack-off parties' in Paris and Amsterdam." Paper presented at the 5th International Conference on AIDS, Montreal, 1989.

Bandura, A., *Principles of Behavior Modification*. Holt, Rinehart & Winston, New York, 1969.

Bergès, O., G. Pelé, M. Pollak. "Jack-off Parties as a Means for Reinforcing Safer Sex." Paper presented at the 4th International Conference on AIDS, Stockholm, 1988.

Bochow, M. *AIDS: wie leben schwule Männer heute?* Berlin, 1988.

Bochow, M. *AIDS und Schwule. Individuelle Strategien und kollektive Bewältigung.* DAH, Berlin, 1989.

Bochow, M. "Sexualverhalten und Lebensstile homosexueller Männer in der Bundesrepublik vor dem Hintergrund von AIDS. Eine Zusammenfassung der Ergebinsse von drei empirischen Untersuchungen." Unpublished manuscript, Berlin, 1990a.

Bochow, M. "Aids and Gay Men: Individual Strategies and Collective Coping." *European Sociological Review*, Vol. 6 No. 2, September 1990b.

Bottzauw, J., K. Hermansen, P. Tauris. "What a Group of Homosexual Persons Know about AIDS and the Risk of Infection with HIV." Ungeskr. Laeger, 1989a, 151, pp. 1918-20.

Bottzauw, J., K. Hermansen, P. Tauris. "Alterations in the Sexual Habits of a Group of Homosexual Persons after Information about AIDS." Ungeskr, Laeger, 1989b, 151, pp. 1920-1922.

Bourdieu, P. *Le Sens pratique*. Paris, Minuit, 1980.

Carreta, R., P. Manzoni. "Amore e Colpa." *Epoca*, February 1990, pp. 6-15.

Cavailhès, J., P. Dutey, G. Bach-Ignasse. *Rapport Gai. Enquête sur les modes de vie des homosexuels*. Paris, Persona, 1984.

CDC Morbidity and Mortality Weekly Report. June 5, 1981.

Coates, T., R. Stall, C. Hoffi. "Changes in Sexual Behavior of Gay and Bisexual Men since the Beginning of the AIDS Epidemic." Unpublished manuscript, CDC, 1988.

Cohen, M. "Factors Associated with Unprotected Anal Intercourse among Homosexual and Bisexual Men." Paper presented to a WHO workshop, 1989.

Cohen, M., P. V. Couturier. "Designing AIDS Prevention Programs on Three Frameworks Explaining Sexual Behavior Change in Gay Populations." Paper presented to the Conference on Sexually transmitted diseases, Chamonix, 1990.

Coxon, A. P. M., P. M. Davies, T. J. McManus. "Longitudinal Study of the Sexual Behavior of Homosexual Males under the Impact of AIDS, (Project SIGMA)." A Final Report to the Department of Health, London, April 1990, p. 63.

Dannecker, M. Sexualwissenschaftliche Studie über das Sexualverhalten und den Lebensstil homosexueller Männer. Francfort. Kohlhammer, 1990.

Dannecker, M., R. Reiche. Der Gewöhliche Homosexuelle. Francfort, Fischer, 1974.

Davies, P., P. Weatherburn, A. Hunt, C. I. Hickson Ford, T. J. McManus, A. Coxon. "Young Gay Men in England and Wales: Sexual Behavior and Implications for the Spread of HIV." Unpublished paper, 1991.

Day, S. "Anthropological Aspects of STD." Paper presented at the Conference on "Public Health and the sexual transmission of diseases." Chamonix, April 23-25, 1990.

Defert, D. "Un Nouveau réformateur social: le malade." Actes, 71-72, 1990, p. 2-8.

Direction Nationale de la Santé et Affaires Sociales, LAV et SIDA dans les services de santé. Stockholm, Socialstyrelsen, 1988, pp. 46-49.

Douglas, M., A. Wildavsky. Risk and Culture: An Essay on the Selection of Technical and Environmental Dangers. University of California Press, Berkeley, 1982.

Dubois-Arber, F., D. Franck. Evaluation des campagnes de prévention contre le sida en Suisse, Cahiers de recherche et de documentation, Institut universitaire de médecine sociale et préventive, Lausanne, 1987.

Duyvendak, J. W., R. Koopmans. Résister au sida: Destin et influence du mouvement homosexuel, Présentation au Colloque International "Sida et homosexualités." Paris, 12-13 avril 1991.

Ebbensen, E. *AIDS in Denmark*, Munksgaard, Copenhagen, 1988.

Emmons, C. A., J. G. Joseph, R. C. Kessler, et al. "Psychological Predictors of Reported Behavior Change in Homosexual Men at Risk for AIDS." *Health Education Quarterly*, 13: 331-345, 1986.

European Center for Epidemiological Monitoring of AIDS, Unpublished Data, Hospital National de Saint-Maurice, Saint-Maurice, 1990 (see p. 65).

Fay, R. E., Ch. F. Turner, A. D. Klassen, J. H. Gagnon. "Prevalence and Patterns of Same-gender Sexual Contact among Men." *Science*, 243, 1989, pp. 338-348.

Fischhoff, B., S. Lichtenstein, P. Slovic, et al. *Acceptable Risk*. Cambridge University Press, New York, 1982.

GHA Survey Results, Special Issue of Aids Action News. August 1989, p. 3.

Gordon, P. "Safer Sex Education Workshops for Gay and Bisexual Men: A review." Unpublished manuscript prepared for the Health Education Authorities, London, UK.

van Griensven, G.J.P., R.A.P. Tielman, J. Goudsmit, et al. "Risk Factors and Prevalence of HIV Antibodies in Homosexual Men in the Netherlands." *American Journal of Epidemiology*, 125, 6, 1987, pp. 25-34.

van Griensven, G.J.P., et al. "Epidemiology and prevention of HIV infection among homosexual men." PhD thesis, Amsterdam, 1989, pp. 41-42.

Guasch Andreu, O. De la "peineta al cuero." Los Homosexuales en la Cataluna actual, Tesis de Licenciatura, Universidad de Barcelona, 1987.

Henriksson, B. *Social Democracy or Societal Control. A Critical Analysis of Swedish AIDS Policy*. Glacio Bokförlag, Stockholm, 1988.

Hirsch, E. *AIDES. Solidaires*. Paris, Cerf, 1991.

Hubert, M. "AIDS in Belgium: Africa in Microcosm." In: *Action on AIDS. National Policies Comparative Perspective*, edited by A. Misztal, D. Moss. Greenwood Press, New York, 1990.

ILGA. *Second ILGA Pink Book*. A global view of lesbian and gay liberation and oppression, Utrecht Series on gay and lesbian studies, no. 12, 1988.

Janz, N. K., M. H. Becker. "The Health Belief Model: A Decade Later." *Health Education Quarterly*, 11: 1-47, 1984.

Jette, A. M., K. M. Cummings, B. M. Brock, M. C. Phelps, J. Naessens. "The Structure and Reliability of Health Belief Indices." *Health Services Research*, 16: 81-98, 1981.

Job, R. F. S. "Effective and Ineffective Use of Fear in Health Promotion Campaigns." *American Journal of Public Health*, 1988, 78, pp. 163-167.

Kelly, J. A., J. S. St. Lawrence. "The AIDS Health Crisis." *Psychological and social interventions*, Plenum Press, New York and London, 1988.

Kingsley, L., R. Detels, R. Kaslow, et al. "Risk Factors for Seroconversion to Human Immunodeficiency Virus among Male Homosexuals." *Lancet*, 1, (8529), 1987, pp. 345-349.

Kinsey, A., W. Pomeroy, C. Martin. *Sexual Behavior in the Human Male*. Philadelphia, London, Saunders, 1968.

Lance, L. "Human Sexuality Course Socialization: An analysis of changes in sexual attitudes and sexual behavior." *Journal of Sex Education and Therapy*, 2, 1975: 8-14.

Lefaure, C., J. P. Moatti. "Les ambiguités de l'acceptable: perception des risques et controverses sur les technologies." *Culture Technique*, 1983, 11: 11-25.

McManus, T., M. McEvoy. "Some Aspects of Male Homosexual Behavior in the UK," *B. J. Sexual Medicine*, 20, 1987, pp. 110-120.

Melbye, M. "To participants in the study by the Cancer Research Institute from 1981 concerning Kaposi's sarcoma/AIDS." PAN-bladet Landsforeningen for bosser og lesbiske, Copenhagen, 1989, 4.

Moatti, J. P., W. Dab, M. Pollak, P. Quebrel, A. Anes, N. Beltzer, C. Menard, C. Serrand. "Les attitudes et comportements des Français face au sida." in *La Recherche*, no. 223, 1990, pp. 889-895.

Moss, D. AIDS in Italy: Emergency in Slow Motion, In *Action on AIDS National Policies Comparative Perspectives*, edited by A. Misztal and A. Moss. Greenwood Press, New York, 1990.

Nelkin, D. "AIDS and the Social Sciences: A review of useful knowledge and research needs." *Reviews of Infectious Diseases*, 9, (5): 980-986, 1987.

Perrow, Ch., M.F. Guillen. *The AIDS Disaster, The Failure of Organizations in New York and the Nation.* New Haven, Yale University Press, 1990.

Pokrovsky, V., I. Eramova. "Sexual Behavior and HIV Spreading in the USSR Gay Population." Poster MD 4117, VIIth International Conference on AIDS. Florence. 16-21 June 1991.

Pollak, M. "L'adaptation au risque de contamination par le VIH." Report to DGS, Paris, 1987.

Pollak, M. "La Diffusion différentielle de l'épidémie du Sida. Une approche sociologique." *Cahiers de sociologie et de démographie médicale,* 28, 3, 1988a, pp. 243-262.

Pollak, M. *Les homosexuels et le sida. Sociologie d'une épidémie.* Paris, Métailié, 1988b.

Pollak, M. "Le gouvernement: zéro!" in *Gai Pied Hebdo,* no. 395, November 1989, pp. 56-58.

Pollak, M., S. Rosman. "Les associations de lutte contre le SIDA: éléments d'évaluation et de réflexion." Report prepared for MIRE, Ministry of Social Affairs, Paris, July 1989.

Pollak, M., M. A. Schiltz. "Does Voluntary Testing Matter?" Paper presented at the 4th International Conference on AIDS, Stockholm, 1988.

Pollak, M., M. A. Schiltz. "Six années d'enquête sur les homo- et bisexuels masculins face au sida." Livre des données, GSPM, Paris, 1991.

Pollak, M., M. A. Schiltz, L. Laurinda. "Les homosexuels face à l'épidémie du sida." *Revue d'épidémiologie et de santé publique,* 34, 1986, pp. 143 sq.

Pollak, M., G. Pelé, Y. Charfe, P. Boisson, O. Bergès, A. Marty-Lavauzelle, J. M. Mandopoulos. "Evaluation d'un dépliant safer sex adressé aux homo- et bisexuels masculins." BEH, 50, 1990.

Prieur, A. *Kjaerlighet mellom menn i aidsens tid.* Pax, Oslo, 1988.

Prieur, A. "Norwegian Gay Men: Reasons for Continued Practice of Unsafe Sex." in *AIDS Education and Prevention, an Interdisciplinary Journal,* 2 (2), 1990, pp. 109-115.

Puska, P., A. Jissinen, J. Tuanilheto. "The Community Based Strategy to Prevent Coronary Heart Disease: Conclusion from the Ten Years of the North Karelia Project." *Annual Review of Public Health,* 6: 147-193, 1985.

van Reyk, P. et al. "On the beat." A report on an outreach program of AIDS preventative education for men who have sex with men, Acon, Sidney, Australia, 1990.

de Rijk, K., F. van den Boom. Psychosociale Hulpverlening AIDS. Vijf jaar hulpverlening door de Schorerstichting, NC GV, Utrecht, September, 1989.

Sasse, H., A. Bigagli, F. Chiarotti, P. Martucci, D. Greco, F. Grillini,. Studio dei comportementi sessuali di un campione della populazione omosessuale italiana in relazione all'infezione da HIV. Rapporto, Centro Operativo AIDS, Istituto Superiore di Sanita, Arci Gay, Roma and Bologna. December 1990. Report 32 p.

Schmidt, K. Unpublished data.

Sherif, M. "A study of some social factors of perception." *Archives of Psychology*, 27, no. 187, 1935.

Siegel, K., P. B. Grodsky, A. Herman. "AIDS Risk-Reduction Guidelines: A Review and Analysis." *Journal of Community Health*, 11 (4): 233-243, 1986.

Siegel, K., M. P. Levine, Ch. Brooks, R. Kern. "The Motives of Gay Men for Taking or Not Taking the HIV Antibody Test." *Social Problems*, 36, 4, 1989, pp. 368-383.

Slovic, P., B. Fischhoff, S. Lichtenstein. "Facts and Fears: Understanding Perceived Risks." in C. Schweig and W. A. Albers (eds.), *Societal Risk Assessment*, Plenum Press, New York, 1980, 181-216.

Tielman, R., S. Polter. "Evaluation of the Dutch AIDS Prevention Campaign among Homosexual Men." Paper presented at the 4th International Conference on AIDS, Stockholm, 1988.

Tielman, R., T. de Jonge. "A Worldwide Inventory of the Legal and Social Situation of Lesbians and Gay Men." in *Second ILGA Pink Book*, 1988, pp. 183 sq.

Vincke, J., R. Mak, R. Bolton. "The Motivational Structure of Risky Sexual Behavior among Gay Men." Poster MD 4053, VIIth International Conference on AIDS, Florence, 16-21 June 1991.

Weatherburn, P., P. Davies, A. J. Hunt, A. P. M. Coxon, T. J. McManus. "Heterosexual Behavior in a Large Cohort of Homosexually Active Men in England and Wales." AIDS Care, 2, 4, 1990, pp. 319-324.

Appendix A:
Glossary of Abbreviations and Acronyms

AFLS   Agence Française de Lutte conitre le Sida
(French Agency for AIDS Prevention).

AIDES   Aide aux malades, à la recherche, information
du public sur le sida, AIDS: support for patients,
research and public information (France).

CNRS   National Scientific Research Center.

COC   National Gay and Lesbian Organization (Netherlands).

DNF   The Norwegian Association of 48 (Norway).

FHO   The United Council of Homosexual Organizations
(Norway).

HBM   Health Belief Model.

HIV   Human Immunodeficiency Virus.

HOSI   Homosexuelle Initiative, Gay Initiative (Austria).

ILGA   International Lesbian and Gay Organization.

IVDU   Intravenous drug user.

KABP   Knowledge, Attitude, Belief, Practice [Survey].

LBL   National Organization for Gays and Lesbians (Denmark).

LILA   Legal Italiana per la lotta control l'AIDS;
League for the Struggle Against AIDS.

NGO   Non-governmental organization.

OAH   Osterreichische (Austrian) AIDS Hilfe.

PWA   People with AIDS.

RFSL   Swedish Federation for Gay and Lesbian Rights (Sweden).

SETA   Organization for Sexual Equality (Finland).

SIGMA   Socio-sexual Investigations into Gay Men and AIDS [Project].

STD   Sexually transmitted disease.

WHO   World Health Organization.

Appendix B:
Homo- and Bisexual AIDS Cases
by Country and Year

(Source: Unpublished data provided by the European Center for Epidemiological Monitoring of AIDS, 1990, Hospital National de Saint-Maurice, Saint-Maurice, France)

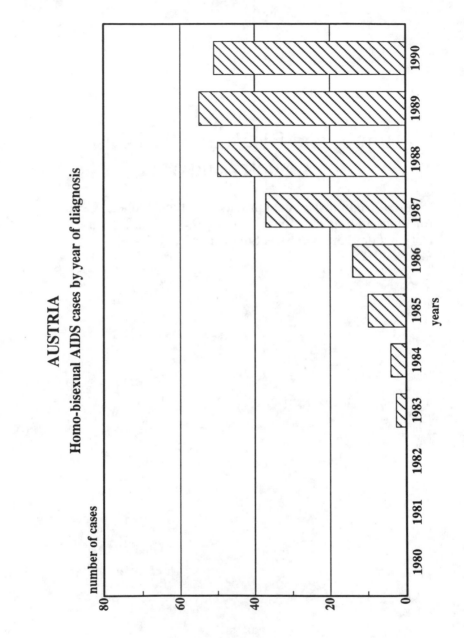

AUSTRIA

Homo-bisexual AIDS cases by year of diagnosis

BELGIUM

Homo-bisexual AIDS cases by year of diagnosis

number of cases

years

DENMARK

Homo-bisexual AIDS cases by year of diagnosis

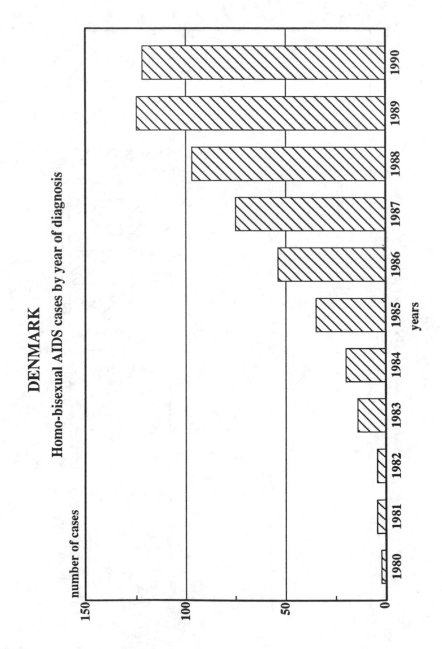

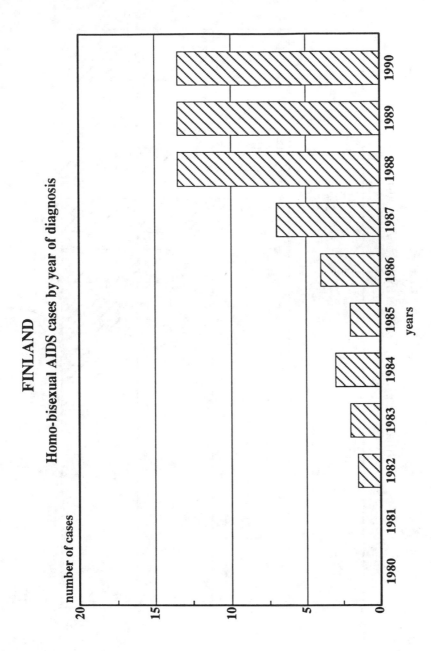

FINLAND

Homo-bisexual AIDS cases by year of diagnosis

number of cases

years

FRANCE

Homo-bisexual AIDS cases by year of diagnosis

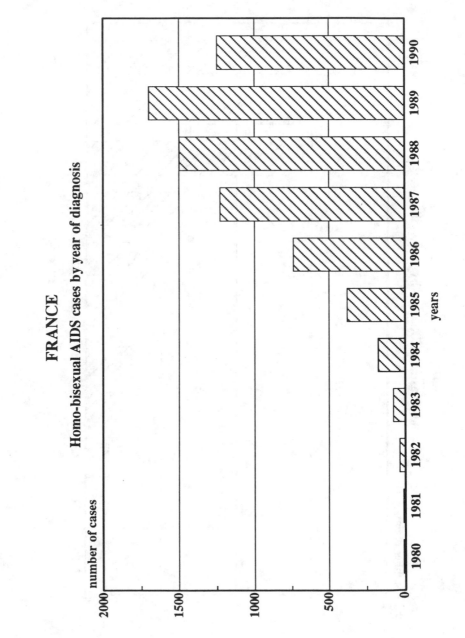

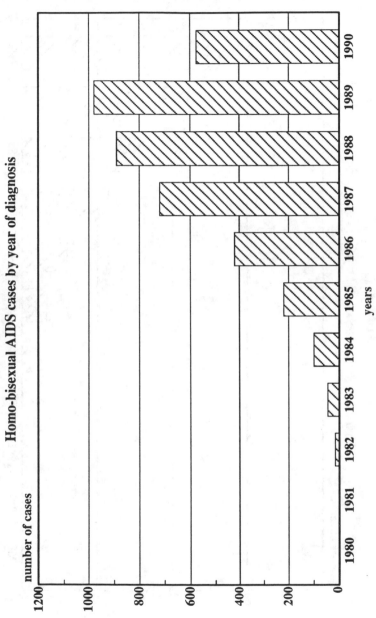

GERMANY FDR

Homo-bisexual AIDS cases by year of diagnosis

GREECE

Homo-bisexual AIDS cases by year of diagnosis

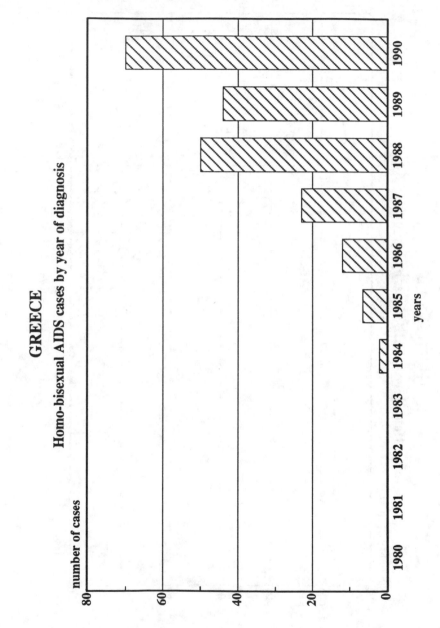

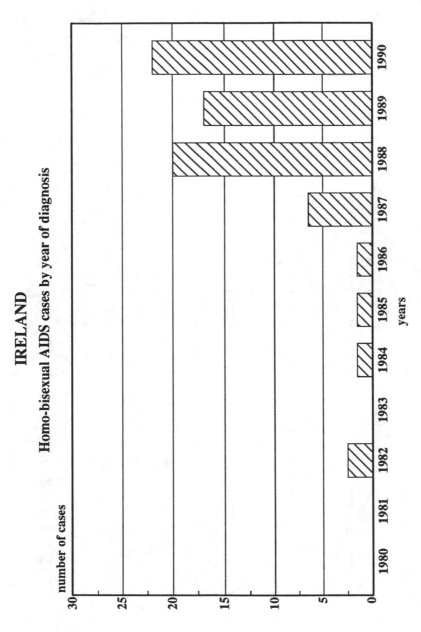

IRELAND

Homo-bisexual AIDS cases by year of diagnosis

number of cases

years

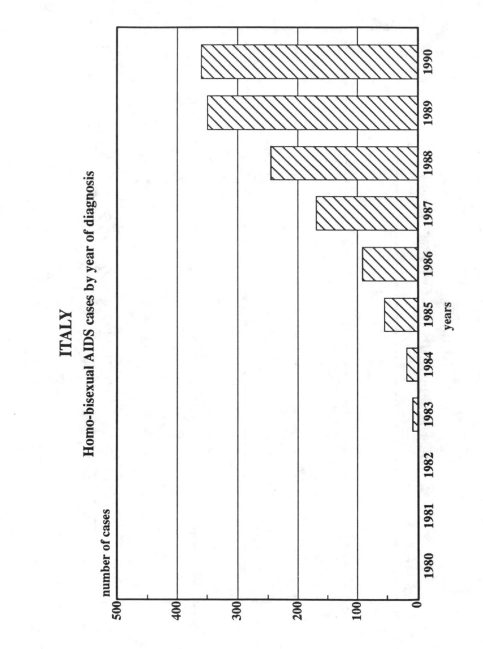

ITALY

Homo-bisexual AIDS cases by year of diagnosis

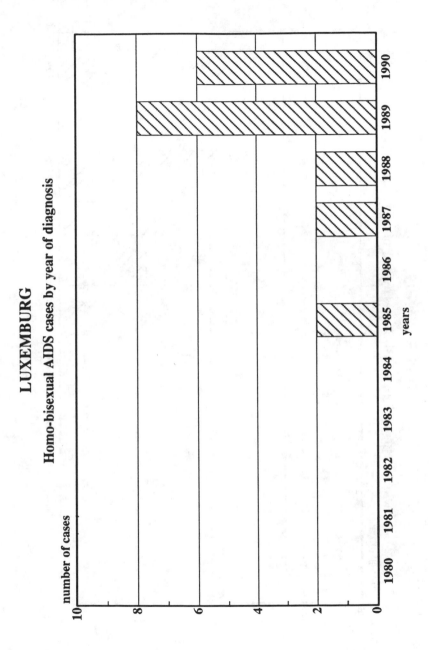

LUXEMBURG

Homo-bisexual AIDS cases by year of diagnosis

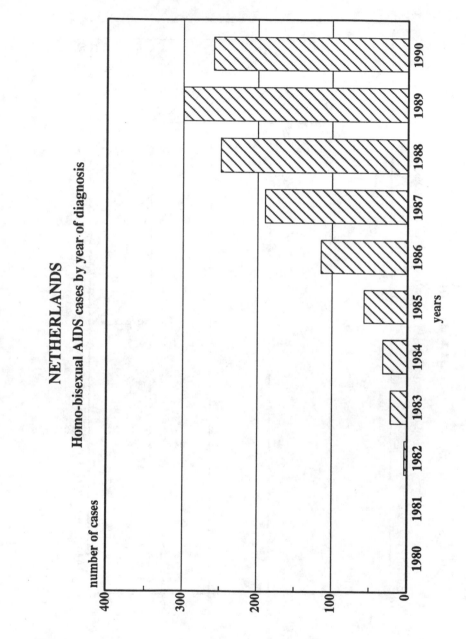

NETHERLANDS

Homo-bisexual AIDS cases by year of diagnosis

NORWAY

Homo-bisexual AIDS cases by year of diagnosis

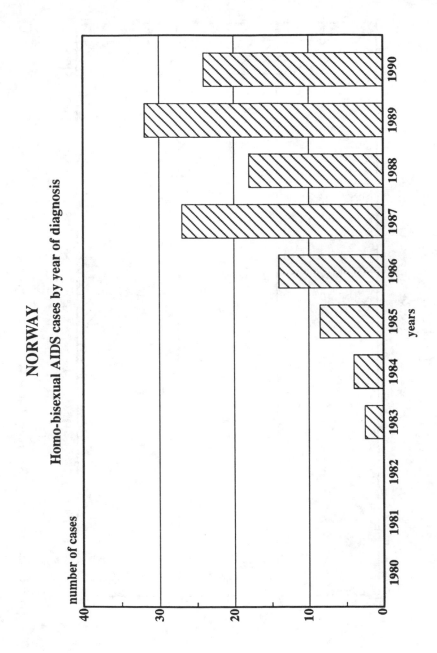

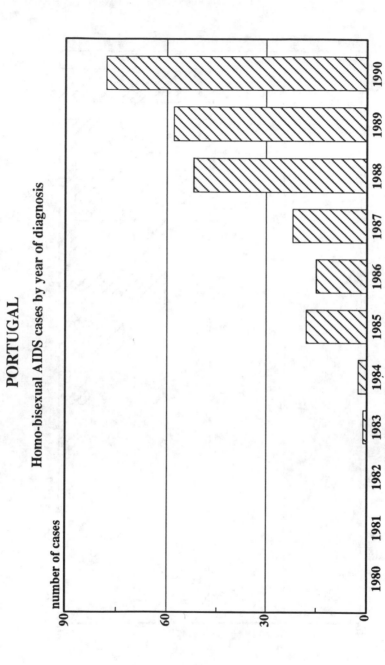

PORTUGAL

Homo-bisexual AIDS cases by year of diagnosis

For 17 cases the year of diagnosis is unknown

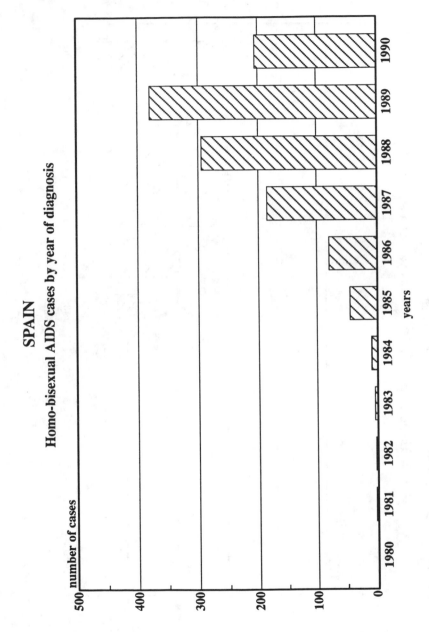

SPAIN

Homo-bisexual AIDS cases by year of diagnosis

For 24 cases the year of diagnosis is unknown

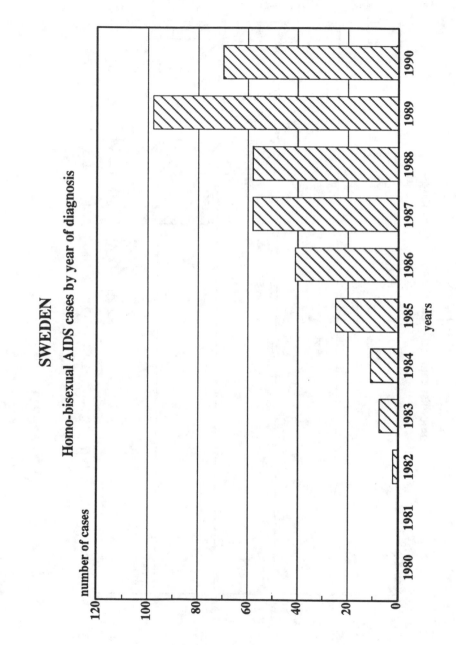

SWEDEN

Homo-bisexual AIDS cases by year of diagnosis

SWITZERLAND

Homo-bisexual AIDS cases by year of diagnosis

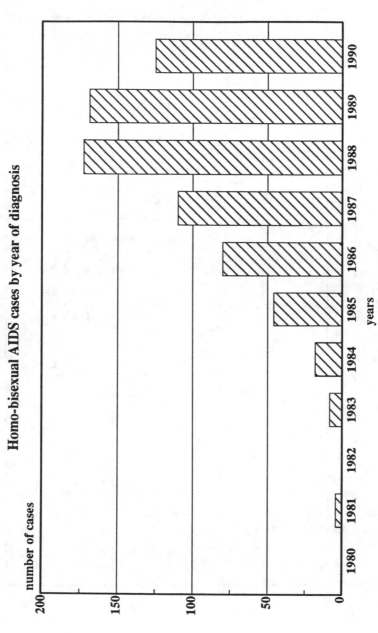

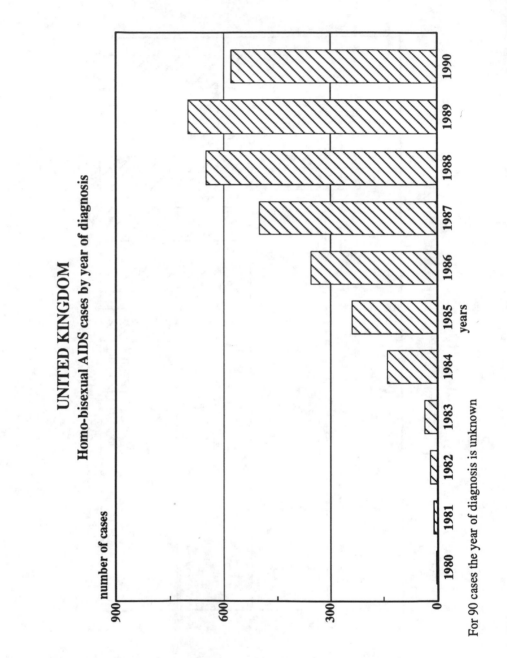

UNITED KINGDOM

Homo-bisexual AIDS cases by year of diagnosis

number of cases

years

For 90 cases the year of diagnosis is unknown

Index